# The Preeminent Person of Christ

A Study of Hebrews 1–10

## Bible Study Guide

From the Bible-teaching ministry of

*Charles R. Swindoll*

Insight for Living

Charles R. Swindoll is a graduate of Dallas Theological Seminary and has served in pastorates in Texas, Massachusetts, and California since 1963. He has served as senior pastor of the First Evangelical Free Church of Fullerton, California, since 1971. Chuck's radio program, "Insight for Living," began in 1979. In addition to his church and radio ministries, Chuck enjoys writing. He has authored numerous books and booklets on a variety of subjects.

Based on the outlines and transcripts of Chuck's sermons, the study guide text is coauthored by Ken Gire, a graduate of Texas Christian University and Dallas Theological Seminary. The Living Insights are written by Bill Butterworth, a graduate of Florida Bible College, Dallas Theological Seminary, and Florida Atlantic University.

**Editor in Chief:**
Cynthia Swindoll

**Coauthor of Text:**
Ken Gire

**Author of Living Insights:**
Bill Butterworth

**Assistant Editor:**
Glenda Schlahta

**Copy Manager:**
Jac La Tour

**Copyediting Supervisor:**
Marty Anderson

**Copy Editor:**
Connie Laser

**Director, Communications Division:**
Carla Beck

**Project Manager:**
Alene Cooper

**Art Director:**
Steve Mitchell

**Designer:**
Diana Vasquez

**Production Artists:**
Gary Lett and Diana Vasquez

**Typographer:**
Bob Haskins

**Print Production Manager:**
Deedee Snyder

ISBN 0-8499-8410-6
Printed in the United States of America.

COVER PAINTING: Nicolas Poussin's *Christ Healing the Blind*, from Kavaler/Art Resource, New York.

# CONTENTS

# INTRODUCTION

The letter to the Hebrews is not bedside reading. Profound and deep, it requires mental energy and spiritual motivation to grasp its contents. But this is not to say that Hebrews cannot be understood. On the contrary, it is a favorite among many Christians . . . often quoted and always appreciated.

These first ten chapters magnify the significance of Jesus Christ. He is presented as the Preeminent One, clearly superior to all other people, created beings, and roles of authority. As such, He deserves our highest praise and our deepest devotion.

At a time when heroes are diminishing in number, it is comforting to know that He can be trusted, that He is our faithful High Priest, that He understands us and has opened the way to God. These and many other truths await us as we work our way through Hebrews.

*Chuck Swindoll*

Chuck Swindoll

# Putting Truth
# into Action

Knowledge apart from application falls short of God's desire for His children. He wants us to apply what we learn so that we will change and grow. This study guide was prepared with these goals in mind. As you go through the following pages, we hope your desire to discover biblical truth will grow as your understanding of God's Word increases, and that you will be encouraged to apply what you've learned.

To assist you in your study, we've included a section called **Living Insights** at the end of each lesson. These exercises will challenge you to study further and to think of specific ways to put your discoveries into action.

There are many ways to use this guide—in personal devotions, group studies, discussions with friends and family, and Sunday school classes. And, of course, it's an ideal study aid when you're listening to its corresponding "Insight for Living" radio series.

To benefit most from this study guide, we would encourage you to consider it a spiritual journal. That's why we've included space in the **Living Insights** for recording your thoughts and discoveries. We hope you'll return to those sections often for review and encouragement as you continue to grow in your walk with Christ.

*Ken Gire*

Ken Gire
Coauthor of Text

Bill Butterworth
Author of Living Insights

# The Preeminent Person of Christ

## A Study of Hebrews 1–10

## Chapter 1

# A LETTER FOR ALL SAINTS AND SEASONS

## Survey of Hebrews

Emerging from the sixties was a generation of kids with long hair, tie-dyed shirts, and tattered, bell-bottom jeans. Almost like people without a country, this disenchanted subculture broke away from the "establishment"—from the business establishment, from the political establishment, and from the established church. They even went so far as to break away from the establishment of the home, rejecting their parents' lifestyles and values.

They were the hippies. Many were bright and perceptive, seeing through the hypocrisy of an adult world that lived behind a veneer of prejudice, materialism, and intimidation.

These American gypsies lived in the streets, in open fields, under bridges. Many experimented with drugs, dropped out of school, and participated in political riots.

But within that strange mixture of humanity there emerged another group—a group that began thinking seriously about the teachings of Jesus Christ. They became known as "Jesus freaks" or "Jesus people." With a guitar slung over the shoulder and a well-worn Bible under the arm, this group sought not a shallow conformity to the church but a sincere commitment to Christ.

One of the popular songs of that era was performed by Simon and Garfunkel. In their song "Bridge Over Troubled Water,"[1] the Jesus generation saw striking similarities to Jesus Christ. How He dried our tears when we felt weary and small. How He was on our

---

1. Words and music by Paul Simon. Copyright © 1969.

1

side when times got rough and friends couldn't be found. Truly He was like a bridge over troubled water. When we were down and out and on the street, and when evening fell so hard, He comforted us and took our part. When darkness came and pain surrounded us, He stretched Himself out, laying Himself down for us, like a bridge over troubled water.

Nineteen centuries earlier, another generation of gypsies wandered like a people without a country—Jews who believed that Jesus was God's bridge over the troubled waters of sin. They were people who were also weary and feeling small. People who were down and out, on the streets. It is to these bruised reeds of humanity that the writer to the Hebrews applies his song as a salve of encouragement.

## Hebrews: May We Introduce You?

Before we take a look at an overview of Hebrews, let's tackle a few introductory essentials.

### Addressee of the Letter

First of all, the letter was addressed to people in a foreign land. They were often afraid, often the object of stares, and often the target of persecution from the establishment of their day. They had placed their trust in Jesus as the Messiah, the only bridge to the Father. But a flood of persecution was rising, and some of them were being swept off that bridge . . . others were hanging on for dear life . . . still others were retreating to the dry ground of Judaism, back to the safe, established religion of their forefathers.

The bridge was a lonely place to stand, because these people, as Jews, were ostracized from the Gentile community. Yet as converts to Christianity, they were also outcasts from the other Jews. Left to fend for themselves, many were without homes, without jobs, without the respect of their peers, and without protection. Separated from the synagogue, they were easy targets for criticism and blame. One such person taking aim was Nero, who ruled the Roman Empire from A.D. 54 to 68.

> In A.D. 64 a great fire broke out in Rome which destroyed a large part of the city. Nero was suspected of having deliberately set it in order to make room for his new Golden House, a splendid palace which he built on the Esquiline hill. In order to divert the blame from himself, the Christians were accused of having caused the disaster. Their attitude of aloofness from the heathen and their talk of the ultimate destruction

of the world by fire lent plausibility to the charge. Many of them were brought to trial and were tortured to death. Tradition says that Peter and Paul perished in this persecution, the first one conducted by the state.[2]

During this time, tension and trauma reigned among the "Jesus Jews." More and more of them decided to follow the path of least resistance, returning to the safety of the synagogue. But then a letter began to circulate. Addressed *Pros Ebraious,* or "To Hebrews," this letter was a song of encouragement, with a few resonant notes of warning, calling them back to the Way, the Truth, and the Life.

### Author of the Letter

The letter had no signature, and it is impossible to say with certainty who the author was. However, hints in the latter part of the letter indicate that those in the author's day knew.

> Pray for us, for we are sure that we have a good conscience, desiring to conduct ourselves honorably in all things. And I urge you all the more to do this, that I may be restored to you the sooner. (Heb. 13:18–19)

Maybe the readers knew his handwriting. Maybe he had ministered to them and promised to write soon, so there was no need to state his name. Maybe he would have been killed had the letter found its way into Roman hands, so he carefully omitted any direct identification.[3]

### Immediate Recipients of the Letter

Although addressed generally to the Hebrews, the letter probably went to a specific group of Jewish believers huddled together in Italy. Chapter 13 provides the hint.

> Greet all of your leaders and all the saints. Those from Italy greet you. (v. 24)[4]

---

2. Merrill C. Tenney, *New Testament Survey,* rev. ed. (Grand Rapids, Mich.: William B. Eerdmans Publishing Co., 1961), p. 8.

3. Some Bible scholars conjecture that the author is Clement of Rome, who was the first person to quote Hebrews in a letter to the Corinthians. Barnabas is also a consideration. And some believe the author to be Paul. All we can say with certainty is that the author is not Timothy (see 13:23). For further study regarding the authorship of Hebrews, consult F. F. Bruce, *The Epistle to the Hebrews,* The New International Commentary on the New Testament (Grand Rapids, Mich.: William B. Eerdmans Publishing Co., 1964), pp. xxxv–xlii.

4. The Revised Standard Version translates the phrase *those from Italy* as "those who come from Italy." "In that case our author is writing outside Italy to a community in

The first place the letter to the Hebrews appears to have been known is Rome, where Clement sent a letter to the Corinthian church in which he quoted from Hebrews.[5] The specific destination of the letter to the Hebrews, then, was very possibly Rome.

### Date of the Letter

Sometime between A.D. 65 and 68, Nero was at the pinnacle of his psychosis, using the carcasses of Christians to light his gardens. The letter of Hebrews was most likely written at the height of persecution, when the storm was raging . . . when the flood was rising . . . when the bridge was slippery.

### Purpose of the Letter

Chapter 2 tells us that these Hebrew Christians were wavering.

> For this reason we must pay much closer attention
> to what we have heard, lest we drift away from it. (v. 1)

It's hard not to waver when the churning water threatens to wash over the bridge beneath your feet. It's hard not to waver when the waves swallow up your livelihood, your property, your children. And these believers were feebly clutching the handrails of that bridge only on the basis of what they had heard. They had no New Testament to which they could moor their emotions. So, as the author of Hebrews sees them slipping off the bridge, he calls out a warning:

> How shall we escape if we neglect so great a salvation?
> (v. 3a)

Later, in chapter 3, he throws these drifting Christians a rope:

> Take care, brethren, lest there should be in any one of
> you an evil, unbelieving heart, in falling away from the
> living God. But encourage one another day after day,
> as long as it is still called "Today," lest any one of you
> be hardened by the deceitfulness of sin. For we have
> become partakers of Christ, if we hold fast the begin-
> ning of our assurance firm until the end. (vv. 12–14)

---

Italy, and sending greetings home from a group of Italian friends who are with him at the time. But contemporary usage does not exclude the possibility that people in Italy are referred to. . . . So far as translation goes, it is best to render the ambiguous Greek by an ambiguous English phrase; so [the New English Bible] says: 'Greetings to you from our Italian friends!' " Bruce, *The Epistle to the Hebrews*, pp. 415–16.

5. 1 Clement, written around A.D. 90.

The Hebrews were weary from treading water in the swift currents that raged against them. To get them back on solid ground, the author admonishes them to return to the rudiments of their walk with Christ:

> For though by this time you ought to be teachers, you have need again for someone to teach you the elementary principles of the oracles of God, and you have come to need milk and not solid food. For everyone who partakes only of milk is not accustomed to the word of righteousness, for he is a babe. But solid food is for the mature, who because of practice have their senses trained to discern good and evil. (5:12–14)

### Style of the Letter

The style of Hebrews is like a well-crafted sermon. It is scholarly, not simple; eloquent, not elementary. It is the type of treatise that would appeal to the intelligent Jew steeped in the Old Testament.

### Theme of the Letter

Throughout the letter, one refrain keeps sounding: *Christ is supreme and superior!* He remains the bridge over troubled water. Even when the flood rises. Even when the winds blow hard. Even when times get rough, and friends just can't be found. When we're down and out. When we're on the street. When darkness shrouds us, and pain surrounds us. That bridge is superior to all our earthly supports. He is sturdy. He is safe. He is Savior.

## Christ: Can You See the Emphasis?

The centrality of Christ in Hebrews can easily be seen by referring to the chart at the end of this lesson. The emphasis is that He is superior and sufficient.

### In every way, He is superior.

Chapters 1–4 demonstrate that *Jesus is superior in His person.* He is better than the prophets (1:1), better than the angels (chaps. 1–2), better than Moses (chap. 3), better than Joshua (chap. 4), better than the Sabbath (chap. 4), and better than all the other priests (chap. 4). This chorus reaches a crescendo in chapter 4.

> Since then we have a great high priest who has passed through the heavens, Jesus the Son of God, let us hold fast our confession. For we do not have a high priest who cannot sympathize with our weaknesses, but one who has been tempted in all things as we are,

yet without sin. Let us therefore draw near with confidence to the throne of grace, that we may receive mercy and may find grace to help in time of need. (vv. 14–16)

The message is, since He is better than all these, we need not drift. Instead, we can turn to the superior one, the High Priest who understands.

Expanding on that idea, chapters 5–10 show that *Jesus is superior as our priest.* He is greater than the earthly priesthood (chap. 5); greater than the Old Covenant (chaps. 6–7); greater than the Mosaic Law, animal sacrifices, and daily offerings (chaps. 8–10).

Finally, chapters 11–13 prove that *Jesus is superior for life.* He is our survival kit for all of life's circumstances. To believe in God, we need to walk in faith (chap. 11). To endure trials, we need to continue in hope (chap. 12). And to encourage others, we need to express love (chap. 13).

### In all experiences, He is sufficient.

Over and over, the author stresses that his readers don't need a priest, a system of laws, or an altar. They only need Jesus. He is sufficient. His once-for-all sacrifice has satisfied God's anger against sin. So in spite of the earthly trials brought on by Nero,[6] they can be assured of their heavenly salvation. But in the meantime, they need endurance to get them through the tough times.

> But remember the former days, when, after being enlightened, you endured a great conflict of sufferings, partly, by being made a public spectacle through reproaches and tribulations, and partly by becoming sharers with those who were so treated. For you showed sympathy to the prisoners, and accepted joyfully the seizure of your property, knowing that you have for yourselves a better possession and an abiding one. Therefore, do not throw away your confidence, which has a great reward. For you have need of endurance. (10:32–36a)

---

6. Nero "had some [Christians] sewed up in skins of wild beasts, and then worried by dogs until they expired; and others dressed in shirts made stiff with wax, fixed to axletrees, and set on fire in his gardens, in order to illuminate them." *Fox's Book of Martyrs*, ed. William Byron Forbush (Grand Rapids, Mich.: Zondervan Publishing House, 1967), p. 6.

The word *endurance* is from two Greek words, *hupo meno*. It means "to abide under." It was used to describe a beast of burden, like an old donkey loaded down with baggage. Even when the load is stacked higher and higher, the donkey keeps standing. He "abides under" the load. That's what it means to endure, to keep standing even when the load you shoulder seems stacked to the sky.

## Christian: Do You Realize Your Need?

As we embark on this new series, we need to realize that we have much in common with those first-century saints who suffered so. Like them, we need to come to grips with the superiority and sufficiency of Christ in our lives.

An old Puritan preacher used to say that there were only two things he needed to know. First, "Does God speak?" and second, "What does God say?" Those questions may not sound very profound, but their answers give light to those wandering in the aimless, darkened streets of adverse circumstances. And Hebrews is just the book to speak to both of those needs.

As you sit and rest a minute at the end of this lesson, you may be identifying with those early Jewish Christians in the first century. Maybe your battle is a physical one and tomorrow looks bleak. You don't quite know what the prognosis is, but you know it's serious.

If so, my friend, what you need is a bridge. The water is troubled, and the bridge is built to get you over it.

Some of you are going through a tough time of disharmony at home. You've run out of answers. And everywhere you turn is just another question.

You need a bridge. It'll take you across those troubled waters.

Some of you are living without any kind of standard, or with the standards bent all out of shape. Your life is in shambles. Maybe you've been on that bridge for years, but you're thinking about jumping off . . . perhaps plunging into an affair or some other form of spiritual suicide.

Let me give a word of advice: *don't.*

If the water is high and the winds are fierce, cling that much tighter to Jesus. Because one day the storm is going to let up. And when it does, the sun will shine again. You'll dry off. And, most importantly, you'll be safe in His arms.

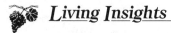 **_Living Insights_**

As we approach this challenging study of the book of Hebrews, the book's theme rings clear: Christ is superior in every way! All thirteen chapters speak to this issue.

- Let's skim the first seven chapters of Hebrews. As you read, try to find an appropriate title for each chapter and list it below. Try to be fresh and creative in your choices; at the same time, try to tie the chapter titles in with the theme of Christ's superiority.

**Overview of Hebrews**

| Chapter | Title |
|---------|-------|
| 1 | _____ |
| 2 | _____ |
| 3 | _____ |
| 4 | _____ |
| 5 | _____ |
| 6 | _____ |
| 7 | _____ |

 **_Living Insights_**

The preceding study allowed us to overview the first half of Hebrews. Let's use this time to complete that research.

- As you scan chapters 8 through 13, look for hints and key concepts that will help you create chapter titles for them, as you did in Study One. Keep in mind this letter's theme: Christ is superior in every way!

**Overview of Hebrews**

| Chapter | Title |
|---------|-------|
| 8 | _____ |
| 9 | _____ |
| 10 | _____ |
| 11 | _____ |
| 12 | _____ |
| 13 | _____ |

# Overview of Hebrews

**Date:** About A.D. 65   **Writer:** Unknown to us   **Theme:** The Superiority of Christ

| Prologue | SUPERIOR IN HIS PERSON | SUPERIOR AS OUR PRIEST | SUPERIOR FOR LIFE | Epilogue |
|---|---|---|---|---|
| "God . . . has spoken . . . in His Son . . ." | **Better Than:**<br>Prophets<br>Angels<br>Moses<br>Joshua<br>The Sabbath<br>Other priests | **Greater Than:**<br>Earthly priesthood<br>Old covenant (Mosaic Law)<br>Animal sacrifices<br>Daily offerings | **Let Us Have:**<br>Faith to believe God<br>Hope to endure trials<br>Love to encourage others | "Now the God of peace . . . equip you . . ." |
| 1:1–4 | 1:5–4:16 | 5:1–10:39 | 11:1–13:19 | 13:20–25 |

| Emphasis: | INSTRUCTION | | EXHORTATION |
|---|---|---|---|
| Key words: | "Better than . . ." | "Greater than . . ." | "Let us . . ." |
| Key verse: | "Since . . . we have a great high priest . . . let us hold fast our confession." (4:14) | | |
| Warnings: | 2:1–4    3:7–4:13 | 5:11–6:20    10:19–39 | 12:25–29 |

# THE LAST WORD
### Hebrews 1:1–3

In biblical times, when God's prophets talked, God's people listened.

The reason was simple. When a prophet spoke, the people knew they were hearing the voice of God. As 2 Peter 1:21 states:

> For no prophecy was ever made by an act of human will,
> but men moved by the Holy Spirit spoke from God.

For centuries, within the ranks of the Hebrew people, no messages were considered more powerful or more urgent than those of the prophets. Warnings and rebukes left their lips like bullets spinning from a smoking barrel. And when they hit their target—the heart—the impact was shattering.

A mere listing of the prophets' names sounds like a roll call from God's Hall of Fame: Elijah and Elisha—the lightning and thunder during the darkest days of Ahab and Jezebel. Isaiah, the princely prophet, who faithfully ministered in the king's court. That is, until the godless Manasseh had him placed in a hollow log and sawed in two.

Then there came Jeremiah with his tears, Daniel with his dreams, Hosea with his heartaches, and Amos with his uncompromising warnings.

And the list goes on. It took the prophet Nathan to slap King David's face and shake him free from an adulterous affair.

It took a prophet named Haggai to motivate the Jews to finish building the temple.

It took a prophet named Jonah to win a hearing in Nineveh that initiated the greatest revival in history.

It took a prophet named John to point an accusing finger at Herod Antipas for his unlawful relationship with his brother's wife.

The prophet was God's mouthpiece—His divine voice box, so to speak. When the Lord had something to communicate, He dropped the mail in their bag. They had one responsibility: to deliver the message, without adding to or analyzing it. As a result, prophets became the most feared people in the community. For it was through them that God spoke.

## God's Message

When we open the letter to the Hebrews, we shouldn't be surprised to find that the first sentence is a comment about prophets.

> God, after He spoke long ago to the fathers in the prophets in many portions and in many ways . . . (Heb. 1:1)

### Long ago . . . the prophets.

This first statement was common knowledge to the Hebrews. It would be like saying to Americans: "Long ago, mail was delivered to the pioneers by pony express." For the Jews, the writer says, God's mail was delivered by prophets. For the sake of emphasis, the writer did not mention the prophets first, but rather the manner in which they delivered the message. The Revised Standard Version captures the proper emphasis: "In many and various ways God spoke. . . ."

A cursory look through the Old Testament confirms this assertion. God's messages were delivered in dreams and visions, by verbal and nonverbal means, through object lessons as well as written communiqués.

The only problem with communicating through prophets was that it was fragmentary. God's message through the prophets always included the implied note: "To be continued." The information was accurate but incomplete—much like the information our parents gave when we were children. If you remember, those messages came in various ways and at different times during our growing-up years. Some were vocal words of comfort or warning. Some were written expressions. Some came in dialogues and discussions. Some through spankings or a firm hand on the shoulder or a hug or kiss. But none constituted our parents' last word to us about life, did it? That's exactly what verse 1 says. There was accuracy in the words of the prophets, but not finality.

A prophet was like an instrument played by the Master Musician Himself. John the Baptist humbly confessed this when he said: "I am a voice of one crying in the wilderness, 'Make straight the way of the Lord'" (John 1:23). As breath is blown through a trumpet and articulated into a tune by the touch of the musician's hands, so the message of God is breathed through the prophet to herald His truth.

### In these last days . . . the Son.

The thought of Hebrews 1:1 continues in the first part of verse 2, where we're told that God

> in these last days has spoken to us in His Son.

Literally, the verse reads: "in the last of these days." The idea here is "at the termination of the times in which He is speaking to mankind." The point is that God's message is no longer spoken through the prophets but through God's very own Son. In the original Greek, the emphasis of this verse falls upon the character or nature of the Son, which colors the contrast a little more vividly.[1] The prophets were merely instruments in God's hand, playing the melody and lyrics He composed. He breathed His truth through them. But when that revelation came through His Son, the composer stepped out on stage and was Himself the message. John tells us the same in his Gospel:

> And the Word became flesh, and dwelt among us, and
> we beheld His glory, glory as of the only begotten from
> the Father, full of grace and truth. (John 1:14)

With the most careful wording, the writer to the Hebrews is trying to demonstrate that *Jesus is superior.* The prophets were the instruments in God's hands, but the Son was the visible presence of the invisible God. When the prophets spoke, they were the mouthpieces. But when the Son finally came, He was the music.

## God's Son

No less than seven facts prove that the Son is not only superior to the prophets but to the angels as well. These proofs fall neatly into three categories.

### He is the sovereign Lord over the universe.

The second half of Hebrews 1:2 reads:

> . . . whom He appointed heir of all things, through
> whom also He made the world.

### The Son is the appointed heir of all things.

The dominion over the world that God offered Adam was dropped from Adam's hands when he fell. But God picked up that scepter and placed it into the hands of "the last Adam"—Jesus Christ.

---

1. Philippians 2:8 has a similar grammatical construction in the Greek: "He humbled Himself by becoming obedient to the point of death, even death on *a* cross" (emphasis added). The focus is on the nature of the death—a cross kind of death. Similarly, in Hebrews 1:2, the focus is on the nature of the revelation—it is a Son kind of revelation.

### Through Him the world was made.

The writer depicts the Son not as a passive tool but an active participant in the creative process (compare John 1:3). The word translated "world" literally means "ages," which is much broader in scope than merely the material universe. It also includes the times through which God's purposes and plans are being unfolded. The Son, therefore, is not only Creator, but He is seen here also as the operations manager, the One engaged in the outworking of events in all of the ages.

Few things are more futile than a philosophy of life that leaves God out. No matter how fervently the scholar or student attempts to give life hope or reason, it is an empty exercise without Jesus Christ in His proper place. It's total futility.

Colossians 1:16b–17 states that "all things have been created by Him and for Him. And He is before all things, and in Him all things hold together." He not only made space, He fills it and faithfully watches over it.

Is Jesus your rock of ages? Is He the center of your past? The center of your present? The center of your future?

### He is the representative presence of the Father.

In the first half of Hebrews 1:3, we find three more points that prove Christ's superiority.

> And He is the radiance of His glory and the exact
> representation of His nature, and upholds all things
> by the word of His power.

The word *radiance* here means "effulgence" or "flashing forth" of the light originating from God. No prophet could claim that. Like the sun in our world, He is the light. The prophets, luminaries that they were, were like the moon, merely reflections of that light.

The term translated "representation" is the word *charaktēr*. The reliable Greek scholars Moulton and Milligan describe this word in their lexicon:

> From denoting "the tool for engraving," [*charaktēr*]
> came to be used of the "mark," "impress" made, with
> special reference to any distinguishing peculiarity, and
> hence [equals] "an exact reproduction."[2]

2. James Hope Moulton and George Milligan, *The Vocabulary of the Greek New Testament: Illustrated from the Papyri and Other Non-Literary Sources* (Grand Rapids, Mich.: William B. Eerdmans Publishing Co., 1972), p. 683.

Jesus is the precise reproduction of the Father's nature. And no prophet could claim that.

The picture of Jesus upholding all things is not of Atlas, passively holding the dead weight of the world on his shoulders. Rather, it is of Jesus actively maintaining the constant movement of events, carrying on their development, and giving them direction and meaning. And no prophet could claim responsibility of that magnitude.

He is preeminently better than the angels.

The latter portion of verse 3 describes the Son as superior to the angels.

> When He had made purification of sins, He sat down
> at the right hand of the Majesty on high.

The Son is superior because He made possible purification of sins. When Jesus went to the cross, He solved the problem of sin (Isa. 53:10–11). Forever. Once for all. And that is something no angel can claim to have accomplished.

Furthermore, the Son is superior because He sat down at the right hand of Majesty. When He died on the cross and appeased the anger of God for our sins, Jesus was escorted by the angels to the throne of the Almighty. He sat down at the favored place beside the Father with calm and absolute confidence. None of the angels had such a position of honor in heaven. Seated, in charge, not needing to explain His actions or the mysterious plan of His glory, Jesus remains superior.

## God's Truth

In the passage we've studied, three burning questions asked today are answered in Jesus Christ.

*Does God still release divine truth?* No. God has spoken in His Son, and there is finality in that revelation. We tend to look everywhere for a revelation from God, not realizing that He has fully revealed His will in His Word. Sure, He gives insight and illumination, but inspired revelation comes only through His Word.

*Has God lost control of the world He made?* If your primary source of information is the morning newspaper or the nightly news, you might get the distinct impression that He has. But when you read the book of Hebrews, you have to answer no. There's a sovereignty in His control. And we can only have peace when we trust that He rules over the rebellion and randomness of this world. In Him we can place our trust, despite any unanswered questions we may have.

Can man know the God who revealed truth and maintains control over this earth? This time, an unqualified yes. Jesus Christ is the exact imprint of the Father. Do you want to know God? Study the person of Christ. Do you want to know how to live? Study the teachings of Christ. Do you want to know how to follow God? Look into the final word from God—the New Testament. He is there, robed in all His splendor and majesty.

 ## _Living Insights_

Hebrews 1 begins with seven facts about the Son of God that prove Him to be superior to the prophets and angels. These seven statements are a fascinating introduction to our God, Jesus Christ.

- The seven descriptions of Christ are listed in the following chart. Let's do a little Scripture search. Can you find other passages that teach the same things about Christ? As you find them, jot down the references on your chart. If you get stuck, try using a concordance; then try looking in a good book on Bible doctrine.

| The Superiority of Jesus Christ | Reference |
|---|---|
| 1. "Appointed heir of all things" | |
| 2. "Through whom . . . He made the world" | |
| 3. "The radiance of His glory" | |
| 4. "The exact representation of His nature" | |
| 5. "Upholds all things by . . . His power" | |
| 6. "Made purification of sins" | |
| 7. "Sat down at the right hand of the Majesty" | |

 ## _Living Insights_

God "has spoken to us in His Son" (Heb. 1:2). There's a finality to this revelation: God delivering His words through His Son. Let's give attention to these first three verses of Hebrews.

- In order to really meditate on the beauty of today's passage, let's memorize it. Try reading Hebrews 1:1–3 aloud six or seven times. Then, see if you can write this passage down. Use whatever method of memorization is best for you. Spend this time in solemn reflection upon the majesty of your Lord.

## Chapter 3

# ANGELS?
# WORSHIPERS OF THE SON
### Hebrews 1:4–14

The subject of angels is an intriguing one, although one about which most of us are largely ignorant. When we think of angels, it is generally in a decorative sense—adorning nativity scenes, motifing Christmas cards, embossing valentines. They seem more of a religious relic than a reality.

But the Bible is filled with actual, not emblematic, angels. Michael, the Archangel. Gabriel, the angel over Israel. The angel of death. Guardian angels. The list is as long as it is enthralling.

But as captivating as the subject of angels may be, it is not the center of attention for the writer to the Hebrews. Rather, it is only a basis of contrast whereby the superiority of Christ can stand out in sharp relief.

In the first part of chapter 1, the writer demonstrates that Jesus is superior to God's human messengers, the prophets. Now he shows that Jesus is superior to God's spiritual messengers, the angels.

## The Son Is Superior to the Prophets

By way of review, you may recall that Hebrews was written to Jews who found themselves hanging on to hope by their fingernails. They were enduring persecution, harassment, and the seizure of their homes and families. Wondering if their faith in Christ was worth the sacrifices they were making, some began to drift. Still others defected. Consequently, the main intention of the writer to the Hebrews was to point them to Christ, to reassure them that the Son of God was worthy of their dedication. Even if that meant martyrdom.

The writer was saying, "Christ is superior. Don't drift. Don't defect. Don't leave Christ. He is superior to the prophets." That's the message of the first three verses. And now, in verse 4, he reinforces that message by demonstrating that Jesus is also superior to the angels.

## The Son Is Superior to the Angels

Hebrews colors in some of the sketchy details we have of angels. Verse 7 of chapter 1 describes them as His "winds" and His "flame of fire"—symbolic of their swiftness and sweeping power. They are labeled "ministers," the same word used later in verse 14, where they are described as "ministering spirits." There are two primary words in the New Testament for service. The one is *diakonia*; the other is *leitourgia*.[1] The former means to render service to man; the latter means to render service to God. In verses 7 and 14, the second word is used.

Angels provide the Lord with every conceivable service we can imagine. They carry His messages and perform His will among us—warning, protecting, helping, and rescuing us. These supernatural creatures do not provide the type of service rendered from man to man. Rather, their service is from heaven to earth, originating from the very throne of God.

But as remarkable as these supernatural beings are, they are dwarfed when placed back-to-back with the Son. By using several Old Testament passages as notches on a measuring stick, the writer shows that Jesus stands head and shoulders above all the angelic beings put together.

### In relation to the Father.

Jesus is superior to the angels because of His unique relationship with the Father. Although the angels are God's servants, Jesus alone is His Son.

> Having become as much better than the angels, as He
> has inherited a more excellent name than they. For to
> which of the angels did He ever say,
> > "Thou art My Son,
> > Today I have begotten Thee"?

1. From *diakonia* we get our word *deacon*; from *litourgia* we get our word *liturgy*. "Diakonia is found 34 times in the [New Testament]. It means service at table in Lk. 10:40; Acts 6:1, etc. It is used in a general sense for loving service in 1 Cor. 16:15 and Rev. 2:19; for loving service through the making of a collection in Acts 11:29" and "for all services in the Christian community in Eph. 4:12. . . . In the [Septuagint—the Greek translation of the Hebrew Old Testament] *leitourgeō* (about 100 times) and *leitourgia* (about 40 times) acquired a clearly defined meaning. They are used almost exclusively for the service of priests and Levites in the temple. . . . In Hebrews and in some Pauline and Lucan passages, the word-group is used strictly in its cultic-sacred sense. . . . According to Heb. 8:2, Christ, as *letiourgikos*, exercises the service of the high priest in the true, heavenly sanctuary." *The New International Dictionary of New Testament Theology*, gen. ed. Colin Brown (Grand Rapids, Mich.: Zondervan Publishing House, 1986), vol. 3, pp. 546, 551, 552.

And again,
> "I will be a Father to Him,
> And He shall be a Son to Me"? (1:4–5)

The woman who sculpts a beautiful piece of stone and turns it into an almost living image with strikingly fluid and realistic features may appreciate the completed work, but it in no way compares to the son or daughter that she bears from her own body. So it is in the unique relationship the Father has with His Son.

### In the act of worship.

There is a second reason why Jesus is superior to the angels, which is found in verse 6:

> And when He again brings the first-born into the world, He says,
> > "And let all the angels of God worship Him."

As soon as the Son was presented to the angels, their spontaneous response was worship. The point is clear: the superior is always worshiped by the inferior. We never read that the Son worships the angels. But we do read that they worship Him. Turn to Revelation 5:11–12 for an example.

> And I looked, and I heard the voice of many angels around the throne and the living creatures and the elders; and the number of them was myriads of myriads, and thousands of thousands, saying with a loud voice,
> > "Worthy is the Lamb that was slain to receive power and riches and wisdom and might and honor and glory and blessing."

Thus, we know that Jesus is superior to the angels because He is the object of their worship.

### In the demonstration of authority.

In Hebrews 1:7, the writer quotes Psalm 104:4, providing us with some more important information about angels.

> And of the angels He says,
> > "Who makes His angels winds,
> > And His ministers a flame of fire."

The writer describes angels as God's wind and fire, using symbolic language to tell of their swiftness, invisibility, and power. But notice what is said of the Son, by comparison. In a series of Old Testament quotes, the writer sets forth one of the greatest Christological statements recorded in the Scripture. Verse 8 clearly calls the Son "God," and states that all that transpires on earth falls under the category of "His kingdom."

> But of the Son He says,
> "Thy throne, O God, is forever and ever,
> And the righteous scepter is the scepter
> of His kingdom. (v. 8)

As the angels are merely ministers of the heavenly kingdom, Jesus is the monarch. No angel ever had a throne. No angel ever had a kingdom. The Son is superior because He has both. His superiority is further underscored in verse 9.

> "Thou hast loved righteousness and hated lawlessness;
> Therefore God, Thy God, hath anointed Thee
> With the oil of gladness above Thy companions."

He is morally superior to His companions, the angels, because He is absolutely righteous. And it is from His righteous character that the creation originated.

> "Thou, Lord, in the beginning didst lay the foundation
> of the earth,
> And the heavens are the works of Thy hands. (v. 10)

Modern science tells us that the human being stands about midway in size in the created order. This means that when compared to man, the atom is as small as the universe is large. That atom, so small that it takes the most powerful microscope to provide even a blurry picture of it, is a solar system all its own with electrons revolving around the nucleus. What angel could have ever been responsible for something that intricate and complex? But science also tells us, by the second law of thermodynamics, that the universe will eventually run down. An assertion that the writer to the Hebrews is quick to agree with.

> "They will perish, but Thou remainest;
> And they all will become old as a garment,
> And as a mantle Thou wilt roll them up;
> As a garment they will also be changed.
> But Thou art the same,
> And Thy years will not come to an end." (vv. 11–12)

Even though everything will wear out like a garment . . . wind down like a tired, old watch . . . wither away like a dying branch,

Jesus will never perish. He is the same yesterday, today, and forever (Heb. 13:8). He is eternal. He had no beginning. He will have no end. And of what angel can that be said?

**In position and purpose.**

Not only is Christ's permanency superior to the angels, but so is His position.

> But to which of the angels has He ever said,
> > "Sit at My right hand,
> > Until I make Thine enemies
> > A footstool for Thy feet"? (1:13)

The Son sits on a throne of righteousness. He will see the day when all His enemies will be subdued under His feet like a footstool. Jesus sits where no angel ever sat, and has a footstool no angel can claim dominion over. But not only is Jesus' position superior, so is His purpose.

> Are they not all ministering spirits, sent out to render service for the sake of those who will inherit salvation? (v. 14)

The angels are not sitting; they are ministering. They are not ruling; they are serving. They are not exalted; they are subordinate. It is true that angels render service of inestimable value on our behalf, yet the Son occupies a place of highest authority. And He alone is worthy of worship.

## The Son . . . the Angels . . . and Us

The angels indeed play an invaluable role in our lives. But to keep them in perspective, it's helpful to note a few points.

- God's angelic servants *impress* us and *intrigue* us, but only God's Word can *enlighten* us.

  Remember our previous study? Jesus is the last word. No longer are angels sent to direct our steps into new fields of revelation. Don't seek enlightenment from angelic sources; seek it from the Word of God. Furthermore, although you may be fascinated with angels, don't pray to them or worship them.

- God's angelic servants minister *to* us, but only God's Spirit can minister *in* us.

  Just because they are spirit beings, don't confuse angels with the Holy Spirit. Angels don't transform souls; the Spirit does that.

He is the *Paraclete*, the Comforter, the One called alongside to help. He is our stability, our comfort, our internal guide—not an angel.

- God's angelic servants protect us *physically*, but only God's Son can save us *spiritually*.

Jesus is the one who comes near and enters our heart when we are saved, not angels. They watch on tiptoes and crane their necks to see, but it is all from afar. And, as the hymnist says, the voices of angels will fade when we are admitted to the heavenly choir.

> Holy, holy, is what the angels sing,
> And I expect to help them make the courts of heaven
> ring;
> But when I sing redemption's story,
> they will fold their wings,
> For angels never felt the joys that our salvation brings.[2]

 ## *Living Insights*  STUDY ONE

Have you ever seriously studied the subject of angels? Angels are an important part of theology. Perhaps now would be a good time to see what the Bible has to say about them.

- The following fifteen references give a good summary of what the Bible says about angels. As you look up each reference, jot down the things you discover.

Isaiah 6:1–3 _____

_____

_____

Matthew 13:39 _____

_____

_____

---

2. Rev. Johnson Oatman, Jr., "Holy, Holy, Is What the Angels Sing."

Matthew 18:10 _____

_____

_____

Mark 12:25 _____

_____

_____

Luke 2:13–14 _____

_____

_____

Luke 16:22 _____

_____

_____

Luke 20:36 _____

_____

_____

Acts 12:7 _____

_____

_____

Acts 12:23 _____

_____

_____

Acts 27:23–24 _____

_____

_____

Ephesians 3:10 _____

_____

_____

Hebrews 12:22 _____

_____

_____

1 Peter 1:12 _____

_____

_____

Jude 6 _____

_____

_____

Jude 9 _____

_____

_____

### Living Insights

The key to understanding angels and their functions is to understand the relationship they have with us as believers. Let's review a little of what we've learned in this study.

• What is the relationship between angels and the Lord Jesus Christ?

_____

_____

• Name some things that angels do for you as a believer.

_____

_____

• Name some things that angels *cannot* do for you. Key in on things that are accomplished by God instead.

_____

_____

Chapter 4

# DON'T NEGLECT!
# DON'T EVEN DRIFT!
Hebrews 2:1–4

If a sailor neglects just a few crucial duties, he can jeopardize not only his own life but the crew, the cargo, and even the ship itself. Say he is too tired to lower the sails or forgets to let down the anchor or neglects to properly tie his knots while mooring the ship to the dock, then the boat will be in danger of drifting.

All sorts of things could happen if he drifts off course. He could become lost at sea and die a slow death of starvation. He could run aground on the shoals. He could crash into the clenched fist of a coral reef, reducing his ship to flotsam and himself to shark bait.

Similarly, neglect of spiritual matters leads to spiritual drifting— at the mercy of the trade winds of prevailing opinion, the currents of passion, and the high seas of stormy circumstances.

The result? A person could float away into some distant harbor, far from the Lord and far from the things that please Him. Or get stranded in the shallows of life, never quite able to get off the sandbar. Or get shipwrecked altogether, with the person going down with the ship as a deep-six statistic.

Those are the dangers of drifting. That's why it's so important not to neglect some crucial things in the Christian life, things that are reviewed in Hebrews 2:1–4.

## A Review of the Church

Not only the past and present, but also the future, include sweeping indictments about the catastrophic drift of the Christian community. Paul warns us of a time in the future when there will be a wholesale departure from truth and morality.

> But the Holy Spirit tells us clearly that in the last times some in the church will turn away from Christ and become eager followers of teachers with devil-inspired ideas. These teachers will tell lies with straight faces and do it so often that their consciences won't even bother them. (1 Tim. 4:1–2)[1]

1. The Living Bible (Wheaton, Ill.: Tyndale House Publishers, 1971).

24

Again he issues a storm warning in his second letter to Timothy.

> For there is going to come a time when people
> won't listen to the truth, but will go around looking
> for teachers who will tell them just what they want to
> hear. They won't listen to what the Bible says but will
> blithely follow their own misguided ideas.
> Stand steady, and don't be afraid of suffering for
> the Lord. (2 Tim. 4:3–5a)[2]

In the present, one has only to read the tabloids or tune in to the talk shows to witness the sad state of affairs in the church. Marital infidelity. Monetary irresponsibility. Ministerial immorality. They read like the headlines at a corner newsstand.

Drifting from the message and morality of the gospel was also a problem in the first century. So much so that the writer to the Hebrews chooses this as the subject of his first strong warning.

## A Reminder of the Context

The warning not to drift, in 2:1–4, grows out of the context of chapter 1. In chapter 1 the writer tells us that God's final revelation has been given in His Son Jesus Christ. He represents God's last word. This makes Him superior to the prophets (vv. 1–2) and to the angels (vv. 3–14). This doesn't mean that the prophets or angels were unimportant. On the contrary, they are His divine emissaries.

> Are they not all ministering spirits, sent out to render
> service for the sake of those who will inherit salvation?
> (v. 14)

God's angelic messengers minister to us who have inherited salvation. The word *inherited* is significant here. W. E. Vine defines the word as "that which is received as a gift, in contrast with that which is received as the reward. . . ."[3] It is human nature to value more what we have worked for than what has fallen into our lap. Because it is so easy to develop a careless attitude toward an inheritance, the writer pauses to include a strong warning for his readers.

## A Warning to the Christian

Notice how chapter 2 flows so fluidly from the context of chapter 1.

---

2. The Living Bible.

3. W. E. Vine, *The Expanded Vine's Expository Dictionary of New Testament Words* (Minneapolis, Minn.: Bethany House Publishers, 1984), p. 588.

> For this reason we must pay much closer attention to
> what we have heard, lest we drift away from it. (v. 1)

The phrase "For this reason" forms the perfect transition. Because our salvation is a free gift from God and because such a gift tends to be taken lightly, a warning needs to be sounded.

The writer makes it clear that the problem is not the lack of knowledge. It's not hearing; it's heeding (see Matt. 7:24–27).

Behind this tendency not to pay close attention is a carelessness due to overexposure. This is stimulated by too much theoretical knowledge not being mixed with practical experience.

If knowledge could be measured in inches and feet, from the beginning of time to 1845 A.D. would be one inch; from 1845 to 1945 would measure three inches; and from 1945 to the present would be the height of the Washington Monument.

This overwhelming volume of knowledge—including biblical knowledge—results in our being carriers of truth rather than users of truth. We hear a great deal, but we don't act on what we hear (compare John 14:15, 21).

An example of this careless inattentiveness to truth can be seen every day on board any commercial airliner. Before the plane taxis off the runway, the flight attendant shows everyone how to buckle their seatbelts, where the exits are, and how to use the oxygen masks in case of some high-altitude accident. Everyone hears her, but how many pay close attention? The problem is, we feel the danger is too remote to warrant our interest.

But the danger isn't remote. We become imperiled when we begin to drift. Consider William Barclay's comments on the words *pay attention to* and *drift:*

> In the first verse there may be an even more vivid picture than there is in the translation which we have used. The two key words are *prosechein* and *pararrein.* We have taken *prosechein* to mean *to pay attention to,* which is one of its commonest meanings. *Pararrein* is a word of many meanings. It is used of something flowing or slipping past; it can be used of a ring that has slipped off the finger. . . .
> But both these words have also a nautical sense. *Prosechein* can mean *to moor a ship;* and *pararrein* can be used of a ship which has been carelessly allowed to slip past a harbour or a haven because the mariner has

forgotten to allow for the wind or the current or the tide. So, then, this first verse could be very vividly translated: "Therefore, we must the more eagerly anchor our lives to the things that we have been taught lest the ship of life drift past the harbour and be wrecked."[4]

Hebrews 2:2–3a flows logically from verse 1.

> For if the word spoken through angels proved unalterable, and every transgression and disobedience received a just recompense, how shall we escape if we neglect so great a salvation?

The argument is from the lesser to the greater. If the Law, given by God's messengers, the angels, proved steadfast and brought grief to those who disobeyed it, how much greater consequence will befall those who neglect God's plan of deliverance that was issued and made possible by His own dear Son.

The issue is articulated in verses 3b–4.

> After it was at the first spoken through the Lord, it was confirmed to us by those who heard, God also bearing witness with them, both by signs and wonders and by various miracles and by gifts of the Holy Spirit according to His own will.

This salvation was first spoken of by the Lord, then confirmed by the apostles who heard it, then passed down to the writer and his companions, with the message borne witness to by accompanying miraculous signs and gifts of the Holy Spirit.

The issue then is not: Do we have God's revelation? The issue is: Are we neglecting it in the way we live?

## A Word to the Concerned

If you've become concerned by the problem of drifting and convinced of its danger, we have a few words of advice worth considering.

First: *Absorbing what we have heard is more essential than seeking something new.* We don't need a new book or a new tape or a new seminar nearly as much as we need to apply what we already know.

---

4. William Barclay, *The Letter to the Hebrews*, rev. ed., The Daily Study Bible Series (Philadelphia, Pa.: Westminster Press, 1976), p. 21.

Second: *Overcoming the peril of drifting requires the discipline of application.* Here are a few thoughts on this matter of drifting and how it leads to neglect. When we're under pressure, drifting starts when we rely on our own instincts rather than on the seasoned truth of Scripture (compare Mark 6:50–52). When making decisions, the currents become deadly because we value human ingenuity and opinion more than God's truth. When battling some turbulent seas in our lives, we are in danger of ending up on the reefs because we opt for what is comfortable, though wrong, instead of what is painful, though right.

Third: *Obeying God's deliverance plan is still the only means of lasting satisfaction in life.* As someone once said, the wind and the waves are always on the side of the ablest navigator. Those whose sails catch the wind of God's Spirit and whose hands are on the helm of God's truth are those who safely find a harbor of peace.

Fourth: *Neglecting God's deliverance plan inevitably leads to inescapable consequences.* Again, Barclay's comments are both pertinent and poignant, forming a fitting conclusion to our study.

> For most of us the threat of life is not so much that we should plunge into disaster, but that we should drift into sin. There are few people who deliberately and in a moment turn their backs on God; there are many who day by day drift farther and farther away from him. There are not many who in one moment of time commit some disastrous sin; there are many who almost imperceptibly involve themselves in some situation and suddenly awake to find that they have ruined life for themselves and broken someone else's heart. We must be continually on the alert against the peril of the drifting life.[5]

 *Living Insights*

It's not easy to stay on course in the Christian life. It's far easier to follow the tides and the currents, to be rocked and tossed by society's seas. One sure way to drift is to set your mind on earthly things instead of on things above.

- To help establish your moorings in this area, turn to Colossians 3 and read through the first seventeen verses. As you do, look for

---

5. Barclay, *The Letter to the Hebrews*, p. 21.

characteristics of a mind set on earthly things as well as characteristics of a mind set on things above. Jot down your observations in the space provided.

| Colossians 3:1–17 | |
| --- | --- |
| Earthly Things | Things Above |
| | |

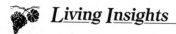

Another way to keep from drifting is to make a commitment not only to *hear* God's Word, but to *apply* it.

• Have you heard or read something recently that you know you need to incorporate into your life? Perhaps a word from our lesson today or from your pastor's sermon last Sunday morning. Possibly it's something you've known you should take care of for quite awhile. Whatever it is, take some time now to think through how you can take it from being a little pinprick of conscience into the realm of discipline and practice. Use the space below to write down your ideas and goals in this area.

**How I Can Apply God's Word**

_____

_____

_____

_____

_____

_____

_____

_____

_____

_____

_____

_____

_____

_____

_____

_____

## Chapter 5

# FINDERS WEEPERS, LOSERS KEEPERS

## Hebrews 2:5–10

Developing the plot of a novel or story is no haphazard task—it takes careful thought and planning. Just look at the way *Writer's Encyclopedia* defines the term *plot:* "the sequence in which an author arranges a series of carefully devised and interrelated incidents so as to form a logical pattern and achieve an intended effect."[1]

Whew!

And just as a serious writer sits down with furrowed brow to plot a novel, so the biblical writer sat down to pen his letter to the Hebrews. Using characters, plot, and theme, his finished product reads more like a novel than a letter.

Its theme of the superiority of Christ runs throughout the book like a dominant thread. And the sequence of the material is carefully plotted, weaving Old Testament motifs into a logical pattern to enhance the main character, Jesus Christ.

But as we read the warning in Hebrews 2:1–4, it jolts us like a chuckhole in the literary road on which the writer has taken us. In the entire book of Hebrews, five of these warnings appear without announcement, making the structure appear rough . . . and the way confusing.[2] But if these warnings are viewed parenthetically, as subplots in the literary text that surface and then quickly submerge, the structure makes sense.

## God's Word and Warning

The readership of this anonymously penned letter was comprised of converted Jews who were in a no-man's-land, unwanted by their families, hated by the Romans, and judged as misfits by the Gentile believers around them. As a result of such rejection, these readers were tempted to drift and even to defect.

---

1. Kirk Polking, Joan Bloss, and Colleen Cannon, eds., *Writer's Encyclopedia* (Cincinnati, Ohio: Writer's Digest Books, 1983), p. 276.

2. These are 2:1–4, 3:7–4:13, 5:11–6:20, 10:19–39, and 12:25–29.

The author's purpose in writing to them was twofold: One, to convince them that their superior Savior was worthy of their trust; two, to warn them that they must guard against drifting and neglecting the salvation God had purchased for them through Christ.

## Man's Dominion and Devastation

If we skip over the parenthesis in 2:1–4, going from 1:14 to 2:5, the flow of the author's argument becomes smooth and seamless:

> Are [angels] not all ministering spirits, sent out to render service for the sake of those who will inherit salvation?
> . . . For He did not subject to angels the world to come, concerning which we are speaking.

In the unfolding drama of redemption, mankind has a loftier role than the angels, because we alone can inherit salvation. Angels have never felt the ecstatic joy that salvation can bring. They cannot enter into the miracle of new birth as we can. At best, they can minister only as midwives.

Not only do angels miss out on the inheritance of salvation, but they also miss out on the dominion over the inhabited earth. That responsibility was delegated to mankind in the mandate of Genesis 1:27–30.

> And God created man in His own image, in the image of God He created him; male and female He created them. And God blessed them; and God said to them, "Be fruitful and multiply, and fill the earth, and subdue it; and rule over the fish of the sea and over the birds of the sky, and over every living thing that moves on the earth." Then God said, "Behold, I have given you every plant yielding seed that is on the surface of all the earth, and every tree which has fruit yielding seed; it shall be food for you; and to every beast of the earth and to every bird of the sky and to every thing that moves on the earth which has life, I have given every green plant for food"; and it was so.

Before the Fall, Adam had not only an undefiled conscience but an undiminished intellect as well. He used that pristine intellect in naming the wide variety of animals and exercising rulership over them.

What a privileged position to be appointed as guardian over all of God's creation. The scope of that dominion is spelled out in Psalm 8, the text the writer to the Hebrews uses to substantiate his argument.

> When I consider Thy heavens, the work of Thy fingers,
> The moon and the stars, which Thou hast ordained;
> What is man, that Thou dost take thought of him?
> And the son of man, that Thou dost care for him?[3]
> Yet Thou hast made him a little lower than God,
> And dost crown him with glory and majesty!
> Thou dost make him to rule over the works of Thy
>     hands;
> Thou hast put all things under his feet,
> All sheep and oxen,
> And also the beasts of the field,
> The birds of the heavens, and the fish of the sea,
> Whatever passes through the paths of the seas.
>     (vv. 3–8)

When the psalmist looked at the Creation account in Genesis 1, he wasn't dizzied by the starry breadth of the Milky Way or awestruck by sapphired depths of the Mediterranean Sea. What amazed him was the quintessential honor crowned upon man to rule such an incomparable domain.

But as we look around to the tattered corners of that domain, we see that weeds have overgrown paradise. We can't help but come to the conclusion that man has clumsily or carelessly dropped the torch that God gave us. That same conclusion is reached by the writer to the Hebrews in 2:6–8.

> But one has testified somewhere, saying,
>     "What is man, that Thou rememberest
>         him?
>     Or the son of man, that Thou art con-
>         cerned about him?
>     "Thou hast made him for a little while
>         lower than the angels;
>     Thou hast crowned him with glory and
>         honor,

---

3. "There is . . . no difference in meaning between 'man' and 'son of man' in this verse. The parallelism of Hebrew poetry requires that the two be taken in much the same sense; and in any case it is quite common in Hebrew idiom for 'the son of' to denote quality, as, for example, 'the son of strength' means 'the strong man.' So 'son of man' means one who has the quality of being man." Leon Morris, "Hebrews," *The Expositor's Bible Commentary,* gen. ed. Frank E. Gaebelein (Grand Rapids, Mich.: Zondervan Publishing House, 1981), vol. 12, pp. 23–24.

And hast appointed him over the works
   of Thy hands;
Thou hast put all things in subjection
   under his feet."
For in subjecting all things to him, He left nothing
that is not subject to him. But now we do not yet see
all things subjected to him.

Presently, creation isn't under the dominion of man. In his commentary on Hebrews, William Barclay comments on this leadership
that has gone awry.

> Man was meant to have dominion over everything
> *but he has not.* He is a creature who is frustrated by
> his circumstances, defeated by his temptations, girt
> about with his own weakness. He who should be free
> is bound; he who should be a king is a slave. As
> G. K. Chesterton said, whatever else is or is not true,
> this one thing is certain—man is not what he was
> meant to be.[4]

As a result of the Fall, man became the loser in every way imag-
inable—intellectually, psychologically, morally, physically, emotionally, spiritually. In taking the fruit from the tree, Adam and Eve
thought they would become like God. Instead, they became less
than what they were.

## Christ's Sacrifice and Provision

But we don't like to admit we're losers, do we? No, we like to
be finders. After all, doesn't the saying go "Finders keepers, losers
weepers"?

Instead of saying, "I've blown it . . . I've dropped the ball . . .
I've lost it," we're more inclined to say, "I'll manage, thank you . . .
I can handle things myself . . . I can get whatever I need."

The only problem is, what gets us through life may not get us
through eternity. Only Christ can guarantee safe passage for that
trip (John 3:16, 14:6).

> But we do see Him who has been made for a little
> while lower than the angels, namely, Jesus, because of
> the suffering of death crowned with glory and honor,
> that by the grace of God He might taste death for

4. William Barclay, *The Letter to the Hebrews,* rev. ed., The Daily Study Bible Series
(Philadelphia, Pa.: Westminster Press, 1976), p. 24.

everyone. For it was fitting for Him, for whom are all things, and through whom are all things, in bringing many sons to glory, to perfect the author of their salvation through sufferings. (Heb. 2:9–10)

By the losers turning to Christ and becoming His children, they become keepers, regaining much of what they lost in Adam. As Jim Elliot, martyred missionary to the Auca Indians, once said: "He is no fool who gives what he cannot keep to gain what he cannot lose."[5] But the tragedy is that there are those today who believe they don't need help from above. They believe they can find help without divine assistance. These are the dyed-in-the-wool humanists.

Humanism is a philosophy that asserts the dignity and worth of man and his capacity for self-realization through reason. And probably no words articulate the spirit of humanism better than the poem "Invictus."

Out of the night that covers me,
    Black as the Pit from pole to pole,
I thank whatever gods may be
    For my unconquerable soul.

In the fell clutch of circumstance
    I have not winced nor cried aloud.
Under the bludgeonings of chance
    My head is bloody, but unbowed.

Beyond this place of wrath and tears
    Looms but the Horror of the shade,
And yet the menace of the years
    Finds and shall find me unafraid.

It matters not how strait the gate,
    How charged with punishments the scroll,
I am the master of my fate:
    I am the captain of my soul.[6]

These are the finders, the ones who reject God's way. They find ways to gain self-importance. They find their own ladders to success. They find ways to gain their own glory. They find ways to champion their own causes. They find their own religion, a religion of humanism in which they rule with their heads held high, "bloody, but unbowed."

5. Jim Elliot, as quoted by Elisabeth Elliot, in *Shadow of the Almighty* (New York, N.Y.: Harper and Brothers, 1958), p. 15.

6. William Ernest Henley, "Invictus," as quoted in *The Best Loved Poems of the American People*, selected by Hazel Felleman (Garden City, N.Y.: Garden City Publishing Co., 1936), p. 73.

But the finders ultimately become weepers, because their own way won't give them entrance into eternity.

> There is a way which seems right to a man,
> But its end is the way of death. (Prov. 16:25)

Unlike the believer who claims, "I see Jesus," the humanist declares myopically, "I see myself!" For the Christian, destiny is restored. The loser becomes the keeper, thanks to Christ. For the non-Christian, hope is lost. The finder becomes the weeper.

In Shakespeare's *Macbeth,* the mournful cry goes up:

> [Life's] a tale
> Told by an idiot, full of sound and fury,
> Signifying nothing.[7]

At the end of life, the living Lord will meet these weepers face-to-face to tell them the lamentable truth: Their lives were a great performance, full of sound and fury and remarkable achievements—but it's all worth nothing.

## Our Hope and Our Choice

The passage we studied today talked about three things:

1. The ideal—what we should be: like Adam and Eve in Eden.

2. The actual—what we are: losers of all the glory we originally had.

3. The possible—what we can be: new creatures in Christ.

As we walk through the passage, we come to a fork in the road where we must make a radical choice: self or Savior?

Choosing self leads only to briers and a jungle of dangers that entangles more and more the further we travel down that dead-end road. Choosing self results in a false hope that emphasizes man's dignity but ignores his destiny.

Choosing the Savior results in the true hope that makes the ideal real. Choosing the Savior leads us down a path that gets brighter and brighter with each day, a path that leads ultimately to "paradise regained."

---

7. William Shakespeare, *Macbeth,* from *Great Books of the Western World, The Plays and Sonnets of William Shakespeare* (Chicago, Ill.: Encyclopædia Britannica, 1952), vol. 2, p. 309.

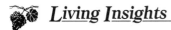 *Living Insights*

One of the best ways to make a point with a Hebrew audience was to quote from the Old Testament. You'll notice that's just what happens in Hebrews 2—the writer quoted Psalm 8.

• It's interesting to compare and contrast Psalm 8 with Hebrews 2. Read the two passages. What is the same in these two portions of Scripture? What is different or expanded? Your study should give you some new insights.

**Psalm 8:3–6 and Hebrews 2:6–8**

Comparisons

_____

_____

_____

_____

Contrasts

_____

_____

_____

_____

*Living Insights*

When you think through this study, it all boils down to two choices: Become a finder, or become a loser. But as our time together revealed, losers actually become the keepers in Christ!

• Let's take time for a little life analysis. In what areas have you chosen Christ as your captain? Write down the areas you've "lost" to Him.

_____

_____

*Continued on next page*

37

_____

_____

_____

- Next, write down those parts of your life you've kept for yourself —those areas you've "found" for self-satisfaction.

_____

_____

_____

_____

_____

Close by thinking through your list and asking God to help you put everything into His hands.

Chapter 6

# PERSPECTIVE ON SUFFERING
### Hebrews 2:9–18

In a simple syllogism, C.S. Lewis articulates the problem of pain:

> "If God were good, He would wish to make His creatures perfectly happy, and if God were almighty, He would be able to do what He wished. But the creatures are not happy. Therefore God lacks either goodness, or power, or both."[1]

To resolve this seeming inconsistency in God's nature, we must view it from a divine vantage point. Then, and only then, will we be able to gain the right perspective on suffering.

One man with such perspective is Alexander Solzhenitsyn. In his monumental trilogy, *The Gulag Archipelago*, he writes of his imprisonment:

> It was only when I lay there on rotting prison straw that I sensed within myself the first stirrings of good. Gradually, it was disclosed to me that the line separating good and evil passes . . . right through every human heart. . . . So, bless you, prison, for having been in my life.[2]

The secret of such triumphant endurance is the ability to see beyond the nearer horizon of hurt to the farther horizon of eternity and to see our own personal pain in eternity's light.

That's perspective.

That's what the first-century Hebrews needed. And that's what we need today whenever the torrents of suffering come raining down on us to veil our view of eternity's horizon.

---

1. C. S. Lewis, *The Problem of Pain* (New York, N.Y.: Macmillan Co., 1962), p. 26.

2. Alexander Solzhenitsyn, *The Gulag Archipelago,* as quoted by Philip Yancey, in *Where Is God When It Hurts* (Grand Rapids, Mich.: Zondervan Publishing House, 1977), p. 51.

## Jesus: Pioneer of Perfecting

The people addressed in the book of Hebrews felt like crumpled-up trash on the guttered back streets of an inner city slum land. It was the writer's intent to pick them up off the streets, to put an arm around them, and to give them a shred of hope to hang on to. That shred of hope was a Savior who suffered on those same streets.

> But we do see Him who has been made for a little while lower than the angels, namely, Jesus, because of the suffering of death crowned with glory and honor, that by the grace of God He might taste death for everyone. (2:9)

"But we do see Him." Perspective comes from focusing on Jesus. In times of grief, loss, tragedy, doubt, disillusionment, loneliness, brokenness, and despair, we will not be able to see the sun beyond those dark clouds unless we fix our eyes on Him (12:2–3).

> For it was fitting for Him, for whom are all things, and through whom are all things, in bringing many sons to glory, to perfect the author of their salvation through sufferings. (2:10)

Jesus is the *author* of our salvation, salvation which He penned with His very blood. The word actually means "pioneer." The picture painted by that metaphor is one of a jungle with the pioneer hacking his way with a machete through the tangled overgrowth to blaze a trail. And Jesus, having cut a swathe through the jungle of sin, stands at the end of that trail, bidding us to follow in His steps.

But to say that the Pioneer of our salvation needs "perfecting" sounds strange, if not heretical. How do you perfect one who is already perfect? Again, perspective is the key. Look at the context. The author is not talking about the deity of Christ, but about His humanity. It's impossible to perfect deity because deity is already perfect, completely free from sin, and completely holy. But the Pioneer of our salvation was perfected, or brought to fullness,[3] in His humanity through the same sufferings we encounter as we walk through life's jungle.

---

3. *To perfect* comes from the word *teleios,* meaning to make complete or mature. The same word is used in James 1:2–4: "Consider it all joy, my brethren, when you encounter various trials, knowing that the testing of your faith produces endurance. And let endurance have its perfect result, that you may be perfect and complete, lacking in nothing." The picture is one of a plant that has gone through the complete cycle of maturity in order to produce fruit.

Those sufferings are what bring us to glory (Rom. 5:1–5, 8:18–25). They are the fires of the furnace that burn away the dross in our lives so that we might come forth as purified gold (Prov. 17:3, Job 23:10). Suffering is the birth canal through which we all must pass if we are to be born into glory. With glory being the light at the end of that dark, constricting tunnel. The pain, therefore, is purposeful as it pushes us out of the darkness and into the light.

## Christians: Subjects of Suffering

In Hebrews 2:11–18 we find at least four areas of pain that force us to look to Jesus for relief and strength.

*The pain of identification.* It was Jesus' suffering that identified Him with humanity.

> For both He who sanctifies and those who are sancti-
> fied are all from one Father; for which reason He is
> not ashamed to call them brethren, saying,
> > "I will proclaim Thy name to My brethren,
> > In the midst of the congregation I will
> > sing Thy praise.". . .
> And again,
> > "Behold, I and the children whom God
> > has given Me."
> Since then the children share in flesh and blood, He
> Himself likewise also partook of the same. (vv. 11–12,
> 13b–14a)

Because of suffering, Jesus can say, "I understand. I know what you're going through. I know how it feels." But just as suffering identifies Jesus with us, so it identifies us with Him.

> That I may know Him, and the power of His resurrec-
> tion and the fellowship of His sufferings, being con-
> formed to His death. (Phil. 3:10)

We have something in common with Christ when we suffer. In the crucible of suffering, a bond is forged—one that draws us closer to Christ than health and wealth and success ever could.

Paul echoes a similar thought in Colossians 1:24.

> Now I rejoice in my sufferings for your sake, and
> in my flesh I do my share on behalf of His body (which
> is the church) in filling up that which is lacking in
> Christ's afflictions.

When we look at pain as a friend rather than an enemy, it becomes something we can indeed rejoice in, for two reasons: one, suffering helps us to know we are identified with Christ; and two, it gives us the perspective that we are merely human, groaning and travailing in labor, waiting for that burst of the new heavens and the new earth when pain will be forever behind us (compare Rom. 8:18–25 with Rev. 21:4).

*The pain of enslavement.* The second realm of pain is found in Hebrews 2:14–15.

> Since then the children share in flesh and blood, He Himself likewise also partook of the same, that through death He might render powerless him who had the power of death, that is, the devil; and might deliver those who through fear of death were subject to slavery all their lives.

Think back to the days when we served another master, when we were enslaved to the devil. For many of us, those were terrible days. Days often filled with pain and misery. Days of disobedience and back talk to our parents. Days of rebellion. Days of revenge. Days of running with the wrong crowd. Days of causing havoc and heartache for those around us.

But when Christ came into our lives, things changed. One of those things was that He rendered the devil powerless—something, by the way, which He hasn't done for angels.

> For assuredly He does not give help to angels, but He gives help to the descendant of Abraham. (v. 16)

*The pain of failure.* There is a third realm of pain noted in verse 17.

> Therefore, He had to be made like His brethren in all things, that He might become a merciful and faithful high priest in things pertaining to God, to make propitiation for the sins of the people.

When we sin, we fall on our face morally. And that tumble hurts as well as humiliates. When we fall, what we need is a gracious hand to help us up, not a harsh foot of judgment to kick us while we're down. Because Jesus was "made like His brethren in all things," He can provide that sympathetic hand (4:15). When He died on our behalf, He became a merciful and faithful priest, intimately involved with humanity and interceding on its behalf (7:23–27).

*The pain of temptation.* The final area of suffering in our passage for today is found in 2:18.

For since He Himself was tempted in that which He
has suffered, He is able to come to the aid of those
who are tempted.

Suffering produces sympathy in us for others.

It is almost impossible to understand another person's
sorrows and sufferings unless we have been through
them. A person without a trace of nerves has no conception of the tortures of nervousness. A person who
is perfectly physically fit has no conception of the
weariness of the person who is easily tired or the pain
of the person who is never free from pain. A person
who learns easily often cannot understand why someone who is slow finds things so difficult. A person who
has never sorrowed cannot understand the pain at the
heart of the person into whose life grief has come.
A person who has never loved can never understand
either the sudden glory or the aching loneliness in the
lover's heart. Before we can have sympathy we must
go through the same things as the other person has
gone through—and that is precisely what Jesus did.[4]

The sympathetic response of Christ to those who are tempted
can be seen in verse 18, in the phrase "to come to the aid." It is
from the verb *boētheō*, which is from the two words, *boē*, "a cry,"
and *theō*, "to run." It means, literally, "to run to the cry."[5]

Whenever we are tempted, all we need to do is cry out for help.
Jesus' ears are tuned to the tempted, and He is quick to run to our side.

## Perspective: Glory of Groaning

Do you know what Romans 8 calls all these painful experiences?
Groaning. Listen to how Phillip's paraphrase puts it:

In my opinion whatever we may have to go through
now is less than nothing compared with the magnificent future God has in store for us. The whole creation
is on tiptoe to see the wonderful sight of the sons of
God coming into their own. . . .
It is plain to anyone with eyes to see that at the
present time all created life groans in a sort of universal

---

4. William Barclay, *The Letter to the Hebrews*, rev. ed., The Daily Study Bible Series
(Philadelphia, Pa.: Westminster Press, 1976), pp. 27–28.

5. A. T. Robertson, *Word Pictures in the New Testament* (Nashville, Tenn.: Broadman
Press, 1932), vol. 5, p. 351.

travail. And it is plain, too, that we who have a fore-taste of the Spirit are in a state of painful tension, while we wait for that redemption of our bodies which will mean that at last we have realised our full sonship in him. (vv. 18–19, 22–25)[6]

Sometimes when the pain is severe, we miss the glory connected with the groaning. Lest we miss it in our study, there are at least three ways that groaning gives us glory.

First: *Our groaning gives us the glory of a compassionate heart.* Compassion is the juice squeezed out of the winepress of suffering. It comes out of us only when we are crushed. And it is that compassion which gives us the capacity to minister to others when life comes pressing down on them. Look at the progression in 2 Corinthians 1:3–4.

> Blessed be the God and Father of our Lord Jesus Christ, the Father of mercies and God of all comfort; who comforts us in all our affliction so that we may be able to comfort those who are in any affliction with the comfort with which we ourselves are comforted by God.

Second: *Our groaning crushes us into the glory of a submissive spirit.* Just as the grape yields to the winepress, so we become submissive when we're crushed. As A. W. Tozer once said: "It is doubtful whether God can bless a man greatly until He has hurt him deeply."[7]

Third: *Our groaning marks us with the glory of a Christlike life.* Nothing is more Christlike than to endure suffering patiently. Look at Peter's cameo of the Cross in 1 Peter 2:19–24, and see if you don't agree.

> For this finds favor, if for the sake of conscience toward God a man bears up under sorrows when suffering unjustly. For what credit is there if, when you sin and are harshly treated, you endure it with patience? But if when you do what is right and suffer for it you patiently endure it, this finds favor with God. For you have been called for this purpose, since Christ also suffered for you, leaving you an example for you to follow in His steps, who committed no sin, nor was

6. J. B. Phillips, The New Testament in Modern English, rev. ed., student ed. (New York, N.Y.: Macmillan Publishing Co., 1972).

7. A. W. Tozer, *The Root of the Righteous* (Camp Hill, Pa.: Christian Publications, 1986), p. 137.

any deceit found in His mouth; and while being re-
viled, He did not revile in return; while suffering, He
uttered no threats, but kept entrusting Himself to Him
who judges righteously; and He Himself bore our sins in
His body on the cross, that we might die to sin and live
to righteousness; for by His wounds you were healed.

That type of patient endurance under the yoke of suffering is
what changes lives. Notice how it changed the life of a nameless
soldier standing watch that fateful Friday on Calvary almost two
thousand years ago.

If it is true that a picture paints a thousand words,
then there was a Roman centurion who got a dictionary full. All he did was see Jesus suffer. He never
heard him preach or saw him heal or followed him
through the crowds. He never witnessed him still the
wind; he only witnessed the way he died. But that was
all it took to cause this weather-worn soldier to take a
giant step in faith. "Surely this was a righteous man."[8]

 ## Living Insights

This is not the type of passage one can read over lightly and
comprehend its meaning; it takes a little more discipline and study.
So let's dig in.

- A very effective tool in Bible study is paraphrasing. It adds depth
and color to the passage being studied, through a more personal
interaction with the text. Let's give it a try with Hebrews 2:9–18.

### My Paraphrase

_____

_____

_____

_____

_____

_Continued on next page_

8. Max Lucado, _No Wonder They Call Him the Savior_ (Portland, Oreg.: Multnomah
Press, 1986), p. 77.

_____

_____

_____

_____

_____

_____

_____

## Living Insights

Our Living Insights are like a journal of our lives. Somewhere along the line pain makes its entry into the diary of our days on earth. Getting through pain is all a matter of perspective. Let's use our time today to make a journal entry based on the answers to the following questions.

- How has suffering given me greater compassion toward others?

_____

_____

_____

- How has suffering produced in me greater submission toward God?

_____

_____

_____

- How has suffering marked me with a Christlike life which I can display to the world?

_____

_____

_____

## Chapter 7

# MESSIAH, MOSES, AND ME

## Hebrews 3:1–6

Christ died not only to gain us entrance into eternity but to ease our day-to-day burdens. And one of those burdens—loneliness—is described for us in Joseph Bayly's book *Psalms of My Life.*

> I'm alone Lord
> alone
> a thousand miles from home.
> There's no one here who knows my name
> except the clerk
> and he spelled it wrong
> no one to eat dinner with
> laugh at my jokes
> listen to my gripes
> be happy with me about what happened today
> and say that's great.
> No one cares.
> There's just this lousy bed
> and slush in street outside
> between the buildings.
> I feel sorry for myself
> and I've plenty of reason
> to.
> Maybe I ought to say
> I'm on top of it
> praise the Lord
> things are great
> but they're not.
> Tonight
> it's all
> gray slush.[1]

If we have placed our faith in Jesus Christ, we not only have a Savior sitting at the right hand of the Father in heaven, we have a

---

1. Joseph Bayly, "A Psalm in a Hotel Room," *Psalms of My Life* (Elgin, Ill.: David C. Cook Publishing Co., LifeJourney Books, 1987), p. 8. Used by permission.

Savior who stands by our side here on earth, even in the loneliest and grayest of circumstances. That was something the Hebrews desperately needed to know, and something we need to be reminded of as well.

## Reminder of the Theme

The theme of Hebrews is like a banner waving over a long, sprawling parade, unfurled high above everything else so that everyone can see it: CHRIST IS SUPERIOR.

He is superior to the prophets (chap. 1) and to the angels (chaps. 1–2). Having come through the crucible of suffering and the jaws of death, this superior Savior is available to help us right now. So to those who find themselves being swept away by some swift current of circumstance, Jesus is there on the banks, ready to throw you a lifeline (Heb. 2:16).

He stands there faithfully and mercifully (v. 17), even during the gray slush days of our lives. That doesn't mean He will blow away the clouds or bring along a rainbow. Not all our illnesses will be healed. Not all our children will be healthy. Not all our ideas will work. Not all our incomes will suffice.

But He is faithful to come when we cry out (v. 18), and He is merciful when He gets here. Isn't that wonderful? God is never so busy greasing the gears of the universe that He can't put down the oil can and come running whenever we cry out to Him.

## Exhortation to the Christian

As we cross the threshold to chapter 3, we step over an important transition—"therefore." It serves to dovetail this chapter into the final verses of chapter 2. The tie-in is with the words "merciful and faithful" and "able to come to the aid of those who are tempted." In other words, based on the fact that we have a faithful and merciful high priest who comes to our aid when we cry out, we are to heed the advice that follows.

> Therefore, holy brethren, partakers of a heavenly calling, consider Jesus, the Apostle and High Priest of our confession. (v. 1)

CONSIDER JESUS—the words are positioned in the chapter like a warm and inviting welcome mat. When we think of the statement in English, the words that come to our minds are blanched: "think about . . . reflect on . . . ponder." But the Greek term for *consider* is much more fresh and colorful: *katanoeō*. It literally means "to perceive down,"[2] which has the sense of "to think deeply."

We find the word in Matthew 7:3, where it's used to describe the scrutiny needed to see the log that is in our own eye. It is also used in Acts 27 at a time of panic on board a ship. When a storm threatens to shipwreck them, the crew scours the shoreline, looking for a safe place to run the ship aground (v. 39). When you're aboard ship with a storm swirling about you, the sea throwing pitchforks of spray, and you're jettisoning cargo as the ship takes on water, there's nothing casual about your looking for a place to dock. Your gaze is focused and intense. And that's the same type of look we should have when we turn our eyes on Jesus.[3]

And what will we see when we consider Jesus?

We will see that He is the Apostle, or literally, "one sent forth," and that He is our High Priest. The Latin term for priest is *pontifex,* meaning "bridge builder." Jesus is the bridge builder between God and man (1 Tim. 2:5), a mediator that Job would very much have wanted in his disputes with God.

> "And I cannot defend myself, for you are no mere man as I am. If you were, then we could discuss it fairly, but there is no umpire between us, no middle man, no mediator to bring us together." (Job 9:32–33)[4]

## Comparison between Messiah and Moses

Another mediator who, in a lesser way, stood between God and man was Moses. He was highly esteemed by the Jewish people, which made broaching Jesus' superiority a delicate subject on the part of the author.

Moses was the mediator who had spoken face-to-face with God, had received the Law, had led the exodus out of Egypt, and had superintended the construction of the tabernacle. To the Jew, it was impossible to conceive of anyone standing closer to God than Moses. Yet someone else did, and that is the point the writer is trying to

2. The Greeks prefixed the word *down* to a term to intensify it, much like the word *up* is often used in English. So the equivalent to devour or "eat up" would be "eat down" in Greek.

3. The word *consider* is also used in Hebrews 10:24—"and let us consider how to stimulate one another to love and good deeds." See also Luke 12:24, where the word is used again—"Consider the ravens . . ."

4. The Living Bible (Wheaton, Ill.: Tyndale House Publishers, 1971).

make in the first few verses of Hebrews 3. In comparing Moses with Jesus, the author brings the superiority of Christ into sharp relief.

> He was faithful to Him who appointed Him, as Moses also was in all His house. For He has been counted worthy of more glory than Moses, by just so much as the builder of the house has more honor than the house. For every house is built by someone, but the builder of all things is God. Now Moses was faithful in all His house as a servant, for a testimony of those things which were to be spoken later; but Christ was faithful as a Son over His house whose house we are, if we hold fast our confidence and the boast of our hope firm until the end. (vv. 2–6)

Note the similarities between the two: both were appointed by God, both were faithful, and both were related to God's "house."

The term *house* is used seven times in these five verses, and the mere repetition of the term tells us it is important. For most people, God's house connotes a place of worship. But technically speaking, the early church never referred to a building as God's house. What *was* referred to as God's dwelling place, however, was His people. We are His house.

> Or do you not know that your body is a temple of the Holy Spirit who is in you, whom you have from God, and that you are not your own? (1 Cor. 6:19)

Not even the ancient tabernacle or temple housed the living God, for it is impossible to contain omnipresence.

> Thus says the Lord,
>       "Heaven is My throne, and the earth is My footstool.
>       Where then is a house you could build for Me?
>       And where is a place that I may rest?
>       For My hand made all these things,
>       Thus all these things came into being," declares the Lord.
>       "But to this one I will look,
>       To him who is humble and contrite of spirit, and who trembles at My word."
>       (Isa. 66:1–2)

An echo of this verse can be heard centuries later in Athens, where Paul addressed the Athenian philosophers.

> "The God who made the world and all things in it,
> since He is Lord of heaven and earth, does not dwell
> in temples made with hands." (Acts 17:24)

As we take a step back from the Hebrews 3 passage, we note some striking contrasts between the two mediators:

1. Moses was part of the house; the Messiah was its architect.

2. Moses knew God personally; the Messiah was God permanently.

3. Moses was a servant in the house; the Messiah was Son over the house.

The author's point in juxtaposing these two? That Jesus Christ is superior even to Moses. "But all that seems to be ancient history," you may say. "How do those facts relate to me today?"

## Relevance to Us Living Today

The emphasis shifts in the last clause of Hebrews 3:6, throwing its weight of application on us.

> If we hold fast our confidence and the boast of our
> hope firm until the end.

The problem centers around the word *if*. At first glance the verse seems to say that if we don't "hold fast," then we're not in His household.

But the writer is not suggesting that salvation can be lost. He is saying that *continuance is the proof of reality*. You want to find proof of the reality of a person's faith? Look at that person's life as a whole, up to the very end. Don't look at a moment of emotional response or at a span of involvement. Look at that life as a whole.

Those who are truly in the household of faith live under the Father's roof and watchful eye. However, they are not immune to flu, failure, or financial collapse. They are, in fact, still very human and very vulnerable.

The main difference between one inside the household of God and one outside is that the one inside has Jesus as his high priest who ministers like no one else can. When the roof caves in, He is the one we can turn to. And when we do, the act of turning is an act of faith that validates its reality.

How about you? Even though you may be in the household of God, the roof can still leak . . . the walls can still collapse . . . the

51

carpet can still wear out. Are you turning to Jesus—our Apostle and High Priest—when life starts coming apart?

He has been sent forth to respond to your cries. He has been selected to intercede as your mediator. When the roof caves in, let Him be the One you turn to.

He can take the rubble around you and, board by board, shingle by shingle, He can start to rebuild your life and make it a house worthy of His presence.

 ## _Living _Insights_

This passage has helped us realize that the house of God is really us. Have you given serious consideration to that concept?

- All houses have blueprints for the proper layout of a particular design. Hebrews 3:4 tells us that the builder of our house is God. What exactly did He build into you? How are you different from, say, a tract house in another neighborhood? What are some specific features in your life which show that you are a custom home, uniquely, fearfully, and wonderfully made?

_____

_____

_____

_____

_____

_____

_____

_____

_____

_____

_____

_____

_____

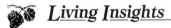 **_Living Insights_**

From time to time we all slosh through "gray slush" days. They're cold and lonely and dreary, and we think the sun will never come out again.

- Describe the last "gray slush" day you had.

_____

_____

_____

_____

- What feelings did you experience that were particularly painful?

_____

_____

_____

_____

- What did you learn to appreciate during that time?

_____

_____

_____

_____

- In what ways did you feel Jesus come to your side when you cried out?

_____

_____

_____

_____

Possibly that "gray slush" day came and went without you ever giving thanks for all you learned from it or for Christ coming to your side to comfort you. If that's the case, take a few minutes now to do so.

## Chapter 8

# BEWARE OF A
# HARD HEART!

### Hebrews 3:7–19

Winding mountain roads are full of warning signs: Watch Out for Falling Rocks. Speed Limit 15. Slippery When Wet.

There are similar warning signs in the book of Hebrews, one of the highest peaks of revelation in the Bible. As we continue wending our way upward through the book, we are periodically confronted by road signs that signal impending danger:

> Pay Attention Lest You Drift (2:1–4).
> Let Us Fear Lest We Fail to Enter God's Rest (4:1–13).
> Beware of Falling Saints (6:1–8).

No one in their right mind would be cavalier about warning signs on a narrow, mountain road. How much more then should we pay attention to warnings on the soft shoulders of the highway to heaven. How much tighter should we grip the wheel. How much closer should we watch the road.

In today's lesson, we will pull over to the side of the road to examine more closely a warning sign found in Hebrews: Beware of a Hard Heart.

## A Backward Glance: The Psalmist Speaks

To the first-century Jewish convert, it would be natural for the writer to subpoena evidence from the Old Testament in order to make his case more convincing. And he does so by appealing to Psalm 95 (see vv. 7b–8a).

> Therefore, just as the Holy Spirit says,[1]
> "Today if you hear His voice,
> Do not harden your hearts."
> (Heb. 3:7–8a)

The original sources drawn upon by the psalmist are the dusty accounts of the wilderness wanderings from Exodus and Numbers.

---

1. The writer regards the words of the Psalmist as those of the Holy Spirit, which is compelling internal evidence for their inspiration.

Both passages look back into ancient Jewish history when those who had experienced the exodus were on their way toward Canaan. The itinerary would normally have taken eleven days but ended up taking forty years.

Why such a circuitous route, when the shortest distance between Egypt and Canaan was a straight line that would have taken under two weeks?

It wasn't because the Israelites had lost their map; it was because they had lost their way. The root of their waywardness was a heart condition. They had hearts that had lost their tenderness and grown tough. Hearts that had lost their responsiveness and become rough. Calloused to God's revelation. Cavalier to His warnings.

Time after time, God put this nation on a treadmill for a stress test. But time after time they flunked the exam. As we look at the electrocardiographs of those tests, we'll see why. The first one we'll study is an internal test, found in Exodus 17:1–7. The second is an external test, recorded in Numbers 13–14.

## The Internal Test

The first test came from within: it was the test of thirst.

> Then all the congregation of the sons of Israel journeyed by stages from the wilderness of Sin, according to the command of the Lord, and camped at Rephidim, and there was no water for the people to drink. Therefore the people quarreled with Moses and said, "Give us water that we may drink." And Moses said to them, "Why do you quarrel with me? Why do you test the Lord?" But the people thirsted there for water; and they grumbled against Moses and said, "Why, now, have you brought us up from Egypt, to kill us and our children and our livestock with thirst?" So Moses cried out to the Lord, saying, "What shall I do to this people? A little more and they will stone me." Then the Lord said to Moses, "Pass before the people and take with you some of the elders of Israel; and take in your hand your staff with which you struck the Nile, and go. Behold, I will stand before you there on the rock at Horeb; and you shall strike the rock, and water will come out of it, that the people may drink." And Moses did so in the sight of the elders of

Israel. And he named the place Massah and Meribah[2] because of the quarrel of the sons of Israel, and because they tested the Lord, saying, "Is the Lord among us, or not?" (Exod. 17:1–7)

The withholding of water was a divinely appointed test. The intent was to reveal the heart of the nation and give them an opportunity to trust that God would provide for them. Unfortunately, the test results were not good. Instead of responding positively, the Israelites turned the tables and put God to the test, grumbling that He had led them into the wilderness to die.

## The External Test

The second test came from outside: it was the test of giants. Shortly after leaving Egypt, the swelling throng of Israelites pitched camp at Kadesh-Barnea. There, God instructed them to send spies into Canaan in a covert operation to determine the country's strengths and weaknesses before they moved in to take possession.

Their report is preserved for us in Numbers 13.

> When they returned from spying out the land, at the end of forty days, they proceeded to come to Moses and Aaron and to all the congregation of the sons of Israel in the wilderness of Paran, at Kadesh; and they brought back word to them and to all the congregation and showed them the fruit of the land. Thus they told him, and said, "We went in to the land where you sent us; and it certainly does flow with milk and honey,[3] and this is its fruit. Nevertheless, the people who live in the land are strong, and the cities are fortified and very large; and moreover, we saw the descendants of Anak there. Amalek is living in the land of the Negev and the Hittites and the Jebusites and the Amorites are living in the hill country, and the Canaanites are living by the sea and by the side of the Jordan." (Num. 13:25–29)

This was God's test. They should have responded by saying, "Look, God got us out of Egypt and gave us water in the wilderness; surely He can get us into Canaan." But they didn't. Notice how they interpreted what they saw in Canaan.

2. *Massah* literally means "test" and *Meribah* means "quarrel." God's Massah was met with the nation's Meribah—His testing resulted in their quarreling.

3. The idea of a land *flowing with milk and honey* is a Hebrew idiom, meaning that the land was prosperous and abundant in resources.

Then Caleb quieted the people before Moses, and said, "We should by all means go up and take possession of it, for we shall surely overcome it." But the men who had gone up with him said, "We are not able to go up against the people, for they are too strong for us." So they gave out to the sons of Israel a bad report of the land which they had spied out, saying, "The land through which we have gone, in spying it out, is a land that devours its inhabitants; and all the people whom we saw in it are men of great size. There also we saw the Nephilim (the sons of Anak are part of the Nephilim); and we became like grasshoppers in our own sight, and so we were in their sight." (vv. 30–33)

Their failure was one of proportion. They saw their enemies all out of proportion to reality. And consequently, they saw themselves out of proportion to their own problems. Instead of an attitude of "If God is for us, who can be against us?" they had the attitude, "If giants are against us, who can be for us?"

With that perspective on their problems, the molehills of resistance that lay across the Jordan loomed ominously before them like the sheer face of Mount Everest. And as they sat shivering at the base of that opportunity to trust God, they blubbered their response.

Then all the congregation lifted up their voices and cried, and the people wept that night. And all the sons of Israel grumbled against Moses and Aaron; and the whole congregation said to them, "Would that we had died in the land of Egypt! Or would that we had died in this wilderness! And why is the Lord bringing us into this land, to fall by the sword? Our wives and our little ones will become plunder; would it not be better for us to return to Egypt?" So they said to one another, "Let us appoint a leader and return to Egypt." (14:1–4)

Again, the Israelites failed the test. And God's response to their failure? It's found in verses 20–23. He tolerated their unbelief for the last time and granted their wish of dying in the wilderness so they wouldn't have to face the Canaanites. Like litter on the side of a freeway, those in that unbelieving generation began to crumble and fall by the wayside, a mute reminder of how seriously God treats the sin of a hardened heart.

Stop a minute to put a stethoscope to your heart. How does it sound? Is it supple and responsive to God? Or does it show signs of spiritual atherosclerosis, a hardening of the heart?

## The Psalmist's Response

Psalm 95 looks back on these twin incidents in the wilderness. With centuries intervening, the psalmist's perspective on the problems Israel faced is the proper one. And so is his prescribed response.

> Come, let us worship and bow down;
> Let us kneel before the Lord our Maker.
> For He is our God,
> And we are the people of His pasture, and the sheep
>     of His hand.
> Today, if you would hear His voice,
> Do not harden your hearts, as at Meribah,
> As in the day of Massah in the wilderness;
> "When your fathers tested Me,
> They tried Me, though they had seen My work.
> For forty years I loathed that generation,
> And said they are a people who err in their heart,
> And they do not know My ways.
> Therefore I swore in My anger,
> Truly they shall not enter into My rest." (vv. 6–11)

The concept of rest is what the writer to the Hebrews takes as his starting point and elaborates on in chapters 3 and 4.

Here's the crucial point to understand: When we're faced with a test that looks insurmountable, God has a rest surrounding that test. The rest is a cease-from-striving mentality, much like the one poetically described in Psalm 23:4—"Even though I walk through the valley of the shadow of death, I fear no evil; for Thou art with me." The rest is like the green pastures and quiet waters where the Good Shepherd wants to lead his fearful sheep. God is telling all of us nervous sheep, "If there's a barrier you can't climb over or walk around, wait for Me . . . rest in Me." "Cease striving and know that I am God" (Ps. 46:10a).

Physically speaking, stress and anxiety are major contributors to a bad heart. The same is true in the spiritual realm. How are you handling the stressful situations around you? Are you resting in Him, or are you restlessly running in circles and raising your blood pressure?

## An Inward Look: The Writer Warns

Returning to Hebrews, we want to take an inward look and learn from the mistakes of the wilderness generation.

The emphasis of Hebrews 3:7–11 is on the outpouring of God's wrath on hardened hearts. Fortunately for us, God's wrath has been emptied on the Cross when it was poured out on Jesus (Isa. 53:10–11). But lest we take lightly the grace that's been given us, the writer to the Hebrews issues a stern warning.

> Take care, brethren, lest there should be in any one
> of you an evil, unbelieving heart, in falling away from
> the living God. (3:12)

The specifics of that warning are found by skipping down to verse 14.

> For we have become partakers of Christ, if we hold
> fast the beginning of our assurance firm until the end.

The verse reminds us that we are not mere spectators of the gladiatorial work of Christ in the arena of salvation. We are participants in the actual working of Christ. And just as it is important for a gladiator to maintain a firm grip on the hilt of his sword, so it is important that we hold tightly to the assurance we have. That's what the Israelites failed to do in the wilderness. They lost their grip on the assurance that God was with them (Exod. 17:7), that He would provide for them (Exod. 17:2–3), and that He would protect them (Num. 14:1–3).

As a result, they failed to enter into His rest, their bleached skeletons ignoble monuments to a hardened heart. But today, we look back on that desert cemetery and two excuses come to our minds. First, we say, "It'll never happen to me." But Hebrews 3:15–16 helps us to take heed lest we lose our assurance and fall from God's rest just as they did.

> While it is said,
>> "Today if you hear His voice,
>> Do not harden your hearts, as when they
>> provoked Me."
> For who provoked Him when they had heard? Indeed,
> did not all those who came out of Egypt led by Moses?

Just as the Word of God comes to us fresh each day, so does the opportunity to harden our hearts against that Word. But calcification doesn't evidence itself when our spirits are high, riding on the crest of some glorious exodus. It shows up in the stress test. It shows up on the treadmill that stretches through the wilderness.

As far as your heart is concerned, it's easier to take oat bran today than nitroglycerine tablets twenty years from now. That's why the advice in verses 15–16 is so good, because it is preventative medicine as opposed to corrective—medicine we are to take *today*, when we actually hear His Word, as opposed to later, after the stress tests reveal a defective heart.

Besides the excuse, "It'll never happen to me," we might also be tempted to say, "I'll wait till later, when it's more convenient." But verses 17–19 answer that excuse.

> And with whom was He angry for forty years? Was it not with those who sinned, whose bodies fell in the wilderness? And to whom did He swear that they should not enter His rest, but to those who were disobedient? And so we see that they were not able to enter because of unbelief.

Unbelief has serious consequences both for the non-Christian and for the Christian. For the former, unbelief bars the entrance to heaven; for the latter, it shuts the gate to the green pastures and still waters of His rest. This is not the arbitrary penalty imposed on helpless humanity by some peeved deity. This is the natural, inevitable consequence of sustained unbelief. Just as hardening of the arteries is terminal if not treated, so is hardening of the heart.

## An Upward Cry: The Lord Lingers

The statistics about the mortality rate from heart disease have shocked people into giving up smoking, adopting a low-fat, high-fiber diet, and exercising regularly. The mortality rate of a spiritually hardened heart should shock us even more and leave us asking ourselves two questions: "How can I keep that from happening to others?" and "How can I keep that from happening to me?"

Verse 13 answers the first question: daily encouragement.

> But encourage one another day after day, as long as it is still called "Today," lest any one of you be hardened by the deceitfulness of sin.

When was the last time you did that with someone? When was the last time you made an encouraging phone call to someone going through the bewildering desert of a divorce or dire financial straits? Reaching out and touching someone is not just a nostalgic, sentimental advertising slogan—it's a biblical mandate.

Verse 14 answers the second question: personal perseverance.

> For we have become partakers of Christ, if we hold fast the beginning of our assurance firm until the end.

60

The perseverance of our faith in testing is the way to enter God's rest. Very simply, here's how it works. Whenever we come to a barrier that creates an inner churning, rather than rolling up our sleeves and resisting, we should take a deep breath and relax. Instantly, we should turn to God and say, "Lord, I don't know what it means, but I take this as a test from You. Give me the heart of a learner and teach me from it."

## A Concluding Word: The Lesson Speaks

Three practical lessons emerge from our study. One, tests come to soften our spirits, not to harden our hearts. Two, rest means that I accept what God wants, not what I want. And three, when resting accompanies testing, divine surprises replace human striving.

 *Living Insights*                                                STUDY ONE

Look back on the tests God put the Israelites through—the internal test in Exodus 17:1–7 and the external one in Numbers 13:25–14:4. Knowing what you know now about the decisions that determined their destiny, what directions would you give them at these two critical crossroads?

Exodus 17:1–7 _____

_____

_____

_____

_____

Numbers 13:25–14:4 _____

_____

_____

_____

_____

Focus on some past crossroad in your life where you took a wrong turn. What decision would you have made then that would have been the greater opportunity to trust God and offered a clearer walk with Him.

_____

_____

_____

_____

_____

_____

Now examine some crossroad you are presently at. What road would be the greater opportunity to trust God?

_____

_____

_____

_____

_____

What is keeping you from going down that road?

_____

_____

_____

_____

_____

_____

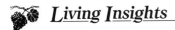 *Living Insights*

Tests come to soften our spirits, not harden our hearts. They come to cause us to look up in trust and dependence, not turn away in resentment.

- How would you describe your present condition?

_____

_____

_____

_____

Are you in a period of testing or a period of resting? Whatever your state, there is a response that is appropriate. That response is prayer. Let's use this time for an extended time of prayer. Talk to God about those issues that are currently important to you. Don't forget to praise Him and thank Him. Create fresh communication with the Father, avoiding the well-worn verbal habits. Make this a meaningful time of confession and celebration.

## Chapter 9

# STOP CHURNING AND START RESTING

*Hebrews 4:1–11*

Two of the top prescribed medications in America are Valium and Tagamet. The former is a muscle relaxant to help people deal with stress. The latter stops the flow of hydrochloric acid to ease a churning stomach plagued with ulcers. If pharmaceuticals are any barometer to where our culture is at emotionally, we're the most uptight, stressed-out, anxiety-ridden culture on the face of the earth.

Why?

Because we've never learned how to rest. Probably because we've never understood what it really means to rest. We tend to equate rest with sleeping in on a rainy morning . . . with basking on the beach, while pouring on the sunscreen and poring over a sizzling best-seller . . . with an afternoon snooze on the couch to the soothing TV background music of marching bands and half-time activities.

But the rest that Hebrews describes is quite different. We don't have to take off work to obtain it. Nor do we need to drive to the beach. Or spend any money.

It is available all day, every day. And it's as close as a prayer.

### Israel's Rest Spurned

The admonition in Hebrews 4:1–11 to start resting grows out of the historical reminder found in the last portion of chapter 3.

> For who provoked Him when they had heard? Indeed, did not all those who came out of Egypt led by Moses? And with whom was He angry for forty years? Was it not with those who sinned, whose bodies fell in the wilderness? And to whom did He swear that they should not enter His rest, but to those who were disobedient? And so we see that they were not able to enter because of unbelief. (vv. 16–19)

That wilderness landscape is not a picture you'd want to hang over your sofa. True, in the background, just over the horizon, there's a land flowing with milk and honey. But in the foreground are the bloated corpses of the hard-hearted. Circling overhead in descending spirals are the vultures. And all the while the blazing sun glares down with its unrelenting and unsympathetic stare.

What a tragedy! And one the author to the Hebrews hopes won't be repeated in our lives.

## God's Rest Offered

It is on the basis of this graphic picture of the consequences of unbelief that the writer issues his warning in 4:1.

### The Warning

> Therefore, let us fear lest, while a promise remains of entering His rest, any one of you should seem to have come short of it.

The Israelites were so close to entering the Promised Land. They stood on the very banks of the Jordan with their toes in the water and gazed upon the cornucopian land. But instead of becoming filled with faith, they became filled with fear. And not fear of their God in heaven, but fear of the giants in Canaan. As a result, their unbelief kept them from crossing that river and doomed them to become dust for the desert.

Just as the gilded land of promise stretched before the Israelites, so God's rest stretches before us as a golden opportunity. But our entering is not automatic.

Before we go any further, let's define what we mean by "rest." The Greek term is a compound word composed of *kata* plus *pausis*. It means "to cease, to stop something." And the way it's used in Hebrews 4, it refers to something that can be entered, like a room or a space. For practical purposes, we might call it *God's specially provided resting space.*

### The Explanation

An explanation of this resting space is given in verses 2–8. And the following subheadings help to clarify that explanation.

*Entering God's rest takes the right formula.*

> For indeed we have had good news preached to us, just as they also; but the word they heard did not profit them, because it was not united by faith in those who heard. For we who have believed enter that rest, just as He has said,

> "As I swore in My wrath,
> They shall not enter My rest,"
> although His works were finished from the foundation
> of the world. (vv. 2–3)

Couched within these two verses is a simple formula: *Hearing +
Believing = Resting.* If we ignore the formula, there is no rest. Preaching the Word is essential, but unless faith follows the hearing of the
Word, the result can be lethal. So just attending a church that
preaches the Bible isn't enough. The hearts that hear must be fertile
and receptive to the seed that is sown (Matt. 13:1–23).

*Entering God's rest takes the right attitude.*

> For He has thus said somewhere concerning the seventh
> day, "And God rested on the seventh day from all His
> works"; and again in this passage, "They shall not
> enter My rest." Since therefore it remains for some
> to enter it, and those who formerly had good news
> preached to them failed to enter because of disobedi-
> ence. (Heb. 4:4–6)

In this section the writer goes all the way back to the Creation
account, quoting from Genesis 2:2. God Himself established the
pattern of rest when He worked six days and rested on the seventh.
The first six days of Creation are marked off by the phrase "evening
and . . . morning" (Gen. 1:5, 8, 13, 19, 23, 31). However, when
we come to the seventh day, there are no time boundaries (2:1–3).
And there is no mention of work on subsequent days. Meaning
what? Meaning His rest from creation continues.

That special rest was never intended to be enjoyed all alone.
God left the gate open to those green pastures of repose for all who
would simply enter in with Him. Just like the hymnist says,

> There is a place of quiet rest,
> Near to the heart of God
> A place where sin cannot molest,
> Near to the heart of God.[1]

However, for the Israelites, the giants that overshadowed their
faith barred their entrance into that rest. And if we're not careful,
our waning faith can magnify the obstacles in our way, making them
appear insurmountable.

---

1. Cleland B. McAfee, "Near to the Heart of God."

Have you entered that rest which the writer to the Hebrews is talking about? Or are you still on the other side of the Jordan, pacing back and forth and biting your nails over the giants that are in the land? If so, isn't it time to stop churning and start resting? Remember that the words of David in Psalm 23:4—"Even though I walk through the valley of the shadow of death, I fear no evil"—were born out of his dealings with a giant. It was David who rested in the strength of God and slew Goliath as the nation stood on the sidelines, wringing their hands (1 Sam. 17:23–24, 45–46).

*Entering God's rest takes the right time.*

> He again fixes a certain day, "Today," saying through
> David after so long a time just as has been said before,
> "Today if you hear His voice,
> Do not harden your hearts."
> For if Joshua had given them rest, He would not have
> spoken of another day after that. (Heb. 4:7–8)

Twice in these verses the writer stresses the urgency of entering into God's rest with the word *today*. Every morning when you awaken to the sun streaming radiantly into your window, God is saying to you, "Today, before your feet hit the floor, start the day with Me."

> "Come to Me, all who are weary and heavy-laden, and
> I will give you rest. Take My yoke upon you, and learn
> from Me, for I am gentle and humble in heart; and
> you shall find rest for your souls." (Matt. 11:28–29).

### The Availability

Possibly you're feeling that you don't deserve to enter into such a rest. Maybe you feel that you need to stay hunched over your anxieties with your nose to the grindstone as you burn the midnight oil. If so, the following verses will be a real relief.

> There remains therefore a Sabbath rest for the people
> of God. For the one who has entered His rest has
> himself also rested from his works, as God did from
> His. (Heb. 4:9–10)

The same rest that God entered into after the Creation "remains" for us. Think of it as a reserved seat in a stadium. As "the people of God," we each have a place of rest reserved for us there. All we have to do is surrender our anxieties, like giving up our tickets to the gatekeeper as we enter the stadium. Just as the football players on the field do all the work to win a game while we watch and rest, so God has done all the work for our salvation and for ensuring our eternal destiny. All we have to do is enter the place of rest.

### The Command

Since entering this rest isn't automatic, the writer issues a strong command in verse 11.

> Let us therefore be diligent to enter that rest, lest anyone fall through following the same example of disobedience.

Why be diligent? Because old habits are hard to break. In fact, some of our worries are so ingrained we almost need treatment at the Schick Center to conquer them.

### Our Rest Provided

Three giants that may stand in the way to our entering God's rest are *presumption, panic,* and *pride.* We become *presumptuous* when we feel we've got things all figured out, when we think we can second-guess God and how He's going to resolve our problems. We become *panicked* when we feel we're not going to make it, when we start seeing ourselves as grasshoppers and our problems as giants. We become *prideful* when we feel we can handle life's problems without God's or anybody else's help, when we look to pull ourselves up by our own bootstraps instead of reaching out to God's hand.

To slay those giants, grasp the slingshot of faith and fill it with three smooth stones of advice—resist presumption, refuse to panic, and release your pride. Once you do that, the way is open to enter God's rest.

 *Living Insights*  STUDY ONE

Here is a good rule of thumb in Bible study: Always compare Scripture with Scripture before checking outside sources. Hebrews 4:1–11 gives us that opportunity.

* Some key words in this passage are listed on the following page. Take a few minutes to get a closer look at them, checking into other Scripture passages that use them in order to gain a better understanding. And don't forget your Bible concordance—it can shed a lot of light on seemingly familiar terms.

## Hebrews 4:1–11

*Fear* (v. 1)               Cross Reference _____

Significance _____

_____


*Rest* (v. 1)               Cross Reference _____

Significance _____

_____


*Good news* (v. 2)          Cross Reference _____

Significance _____

_____


*Faith* (v. 2)             Cross Reference _____

Significance _____

_____


*Wrath* (v. 3)             Cross Reference _____

Significance _____

_____


*Seventh day* (v. 4)        Cross Reference _____

Significance _____

_____


*Works* (v. 4)             Cross Reference _____

Significance _____

_____


*Preached* (v. 6)          Cross Reference _____

Significance _____

_____

*Disobedience* (v. 6)    Cross Reference _____

Significance _____

_____


*Today* (v. 7)    Cross Reference _____

Significance _____

_____


*Harden your hearts* (v. 7)    Cross Reference _____

Significance _____

_____


*Sabbath* (v. 9)    Cross Reference _____

Significance _____

_____


*Diligent* (v. 11)    Cross Reference _____

Significance _____

_____


*Example* (v. 11)    Cross Reference _____

Significance _____

_____

 *Living Insights*    STUDY TWO

Have you stopped churning and started resting? One of the most enjoyable expressions of an attitude of rest is singing.˙

• There are so many psalms, hymns, and spiritual songs that speak about resting. Why not pick out a few of your favorites and spend some time in praise to the Lord? Sing it out, whether alone or along with a group. Make a joyful noise!

Chapter 10

# SPIRITUAL SURGERY

*Hebrews 4:12–13*

In our previous study we found that there is a place of rest divinely prepared for us. It is analogous to the Sabbath rest that God entered into on the seventh day, after He had completed His creative work.

The one obstacle that stands in the way to our entering that rest is the condition of our heart. A hardened heart with arteries clogged by unbelief is going to be distracted with presumption, distraught with panic, and distended with pride. Any of these conditions is grave enough to keep us from entering the rest God has prepared for us.

Unfortunately, there is no medication that can soften a hard heart. There are no triple bypasses in the spiritual realm. The only surgical option available is a transplant. If we are to have a new heart, God must be the one to give it to us (Ps. 51:10).

So with that in mind, we need to crawl up on the gurney and let God wheel us into His operating room. And there, under the intense light, we should bare our chest to His scalpel—the incisive Word of God.

## The Importance of Resting

Our passage in today's study—Hebrews 4:12–13—stands out in its context like a roadblock that interrupts the natural flow of traffic. The entire chapter thus far has dealt with the importance of God's rest and has moved along smoothly. When we come to verses 12–13, however, we screech our tires and stop to scratch our heads.

The problem is not in the verses' placement within the context; the problem is that there have been no road signs to warn us that the subject of God's Word lies just around the corner.

What we need is a transition. Perhaps adding this one between verses 11 and 12 would keep the progression of thought running smoothly: *Mental habits and traditional thought patterns enslave us and keep us from resting; therefore, we need God's truth to free us from that bondage.*

The *presumption*—assuming how God will work; the *panic*—feeling an overwhelming fright that God is not involved; and the *pride*—holding the inflated opinion that we can handle this ourselves. These are all habitual thought patterns that take us down the wrong road, away from God's resting place. That's why the Word is so important. It closes those old mental detours and puts us back on the road to His rest.

## The Process of Rest Applied

Now that we understand the importance of resting, we need a little insight into how to apply that rest. We need to understand the role of God's Word in ushering it in.

### God's truth is effective.

All of us travel through life with blind spots. That's why we need rearview mirrors that enable us to see passing traffic and other dangers we would not see otherwise.

Scripture functions a lot like those mirrors. It provides a clear picture of what's going on in our lives.

> For the word of God is living and active and sharper than any two-edged sword, and piercing as far as the division of soul and spirit, of both joints and marrow, and able to judge the thoughts and intentions of the heart. (v. 12)

This one verse tells us volumes about the Word of God—about its identity, its characteristics, and its abilities.

*Its identity.* The phrase "the word of God" refers specifically to the Bible. But in a broader, nontechnical sense, the Word of God includes anything that God utters and anything or anyone through whom He speaks. So when a counselor gives biblically based advice and God uses that to lance a festering emotional wound, the Word of God has done its work. When a song sung to biblical lyrics echoes through an auditorium, it is the Word of God that is being heard. Regardless of the vessel it is poured from, the water is the same refreshing, life-giving Word of God. See how Paul concurs in 1 Thessalonians 2:13 regarding his own preaching.

> And for this reason we also constantly thank God that when you received from us the word of God's message, you accepted it not as the word of men, but for what it really is, the word of God, which also performs its work in you who believe.

"His preaching was not the outgrowth of personal philosophical meanderings, but was deeply rooted in a message given by God himself. . . . Once received, this Word of God becomes an active power operating continually in the believer's life."[1]

*Its characteristics.* Look closely at Hebrews 4:12, and you will find three salient characteristics of the Word of God.

First: *It is living.*[2] The Word is alive. Like an acorn that has within it a thousand forests, so the Word of God lies in the pages of Scripture like dormant seed within a silo, awaiting only a diligent sower to spread it and a fertile heart to receive it (compare Matt. 13:1–23 with Rom. 10:8–15).

Second: *It is active.* The Greek word translated "active" is *energēs,* from which we get the word *energy.* The Word of God is dynamic. It has energy. It does things nothing else can do. It touches us where nothing else can reach. News articles may inform us. Novels may inspire us. Poetry may enrapture us. But only the living, active Word of God can transform us.[3]

Third: *It is sharp.* How sharp? *"Sharper* than any two-edged sword." The Word of God has an edge to it. It's not a blunt instrument with which we bludgeon our opposition; rather, it has a keen edge that knifes its way into the innermost recesses, where no surgeon's scalpel can go.

*Its abilities.* Two abilities of the Word of God are mentioned in Hebrews 4:12.

First: *It has the ability to pierce.* The word means "to go through something." Unfortunately, even the most eminent of medical surgeons can't operate on the soul. No surgical technique can correct a bad attitude, a closed mind, a rebellious spirit, a lustful heart, hypocrisy, greed, hatred, or an unforgiving spirit. These are all spiritual problems and must be dealt with by spiritual means. That's

---

1. Robert L. Thomas, "1 Thessalonians," *The Expositor's Bible Commentary,* gen. ed. Frank E. Gaebelein (Grand Rapids, Mich.: Zondervan Publishing House, 1978), vol. 11, p. 257.

2. See Acts 7:38, "living oracles," and 1 Peter 1:23, "the living and abiding word of God."

3. "The essential character of the word of God in its inexhaustible vitality and dynamic efficacy is clearly defined in Isaiah 55:11, where God says through his prophet: 'so shall my word be that goes forth from my mouth; it shall not return to me empty, but it shall accomplish that which I purpose, and prosper in the thing for which I sent it.' The vigor and the potency of his word are seen in its operation as his creating word (Gen. 1:3ff.; Heb. 11:3), his sustaining word (Heb. 1:3), and his regenerating word (2 Cor. 4:6; 1 Pet. 1:23)." Philip Edgcumbe Hughes, *A Commentary on the Epistle to the Hebrews* (Grand Rapids, Mich.: William B. Eerdmans Publishing Co., 1977), p. 164.

where the Word of God comes in and does its work. One of the things that sets Jesus apart from other religious teachers is that He spoke the Word of God. Not the words of rabbinic tradition. Not the words of contemporary philosophy. But the incisive Word of God that cuts deep into the marrow of the soul (Matt. 7:28–29; John 8:45–46).

Second: *It has the ability to judge.* The Greek word is *kritikos.* It literally means "to sift out, analyze, scrutinize." We get our words *critical* and *critic* from it. The Word functions like an X ray that enables a doctor to see beyond what any picture could ever show. It is through the deep, penetrating ability of the Word of God that our innermost thoughts and intentions are revealed[4]—as was the case with the woman Jesus met at the well: "Come, see a man who told me all the things that I have done" (John 4:29).

Some of us today have a great deal of trouble resting in the Lord. Often we don't even know why. But there is a desire within our souls that says, "I want that rest. I need it. I must find relief to this churning and stress. But I just can't seem to enter into it." One of the reasons we can't experience that rest is that we have a tendency to hide from the truth. That's where the Word of God comes into the picture—to open our hearts to the truth by its piercing revelations.

### Our hiding is futile.

When we fear that things are not quite right with us physically, an interesting phenomenon often occurs: we put off going to the doctor, the very one who could help us. Mainly because we don't want to hear bad news. We don't want to face the truth about ourselves because it's painful, and because we fear surgery and shots. The same is true spiritually, which is precisely why the writer wrote verse 13.

> And there is no creature hidden from His sight, but all things are open and laid bare to the eyes of Him with whom we have to do.

Verse 13 is an encapsulation of Psalm 139:1–13, where we see God producing His *magnum opus* in the cramped workshop of a pitch-black womb. From such an almighty God, nothing can be hidden—not even the dark secrets of our heart.

Two thoughts emerge from our understanding of Hebrews 4:13. One, *God's Word has a universal scope. No* creature is hidden from

4. The "thoughts" include our deepest feelings and desires, our instincts and our passions. The "intentions" focus more on the intellectual part of us and include our motives.

His sight, not one. Not even so much as a sparrow (Matt. 10:29). Second, *to God's eyes, there is unlimited exposure.* Notice the key terms "open" and "laid bare" in Hebrews 4:13.

The first term means "uncovered" and is used in 1 Corinthians 15:37 for a bare kernel of grain. In Acts 19:16 the same word is used to describe people who are naked. Before God we all stand naked and exposed. We have no cloak for our souls.

The second term, "laid bare," is from the Greek word *trachēlos,* from which we get our word *trachea,* which means "throat." Wrestlers in biblical times had a certain hold that involved seizing an opponent and twisting the neck so as to render him powerless, and the term *trachēlos* was used to describe it. The term was also used to describe the pulling back of the head of a sacrificial animal before slitting its throat, and of a criminal being led away to execution. A sharp dagger was fixed to the criminal's throat with the point touching his chin; that way he was forced to hold his head up, instead of bowing to conceal it in shame. The picture is of a criminal having to face God in heaven without being able to look away from His presence. So the word connotes not only exposure, but also accountability.

### Two Practical Suggestions

To put a practical edge on what we've been studying, let's leave with two practical suggestions. First, *submit to surgery.* Second, *don't fight the physician.* Don't put yourself in a position of giving the doctor advice, telling the Lord where to cut and how deep and what to take out. Trust Him every bit as much as you would the best surgeon. He's going to cut where it hurts, so don't kick or scream or slap His hand away. Remember, He's cutting because He wants you whole and healthy. Because He loves you.

 *Living Insights*

American Christians probably take their Bibles for granted more than any other people in the world. When was the last time you really thought about the valuable treasure in your possession?

- The Bible describes itself in many different ways. Hebrews 4:12 calls the Scriptures living, active, sharper than any two-edged sword. How many descriptions can you think of for the Word of God that come from the Bible? Add those descriptions and references to the following chart.

| The Word Describing the Word | |
|---|---|
| Description | Reference |
| Living | Heb. 4:12 |
| Active | Heb. 4:12 |
| Sharper than any two-edged sword | Heb. 4:12 |
| | |

 *Living Insights*

God works powerfully in our lives, but He doesn't always work alone. Counsel that comes through a person under the power of the Holy Spirit can penetrate deeply into our lives.

- Does God use someone to cut into your life and perform necessary surgeries? Do you have someone to whom you are accountable, with whom you meet regularly for the express purpose of learning and growing? If not, spend some time now thinking and praying about the right person to provide this accountablity in your life.

## Chapter 11

# A HEAVENLY PRIEST FOR A NEEDY PEOPLE

### Hebrews 4:14–16

The Reformation was like a torrential gale that swept over the ruffled harbor of Catholicism. The turbulence was caused by men who were determined to bring religious reform to the Church of Rome by teaching the pure truth of Scripture.

These champions of biblical truth caused more than a tempest in the ecclesiastical teapot. They stirred up a storm with the most powerful dignitaries in all of Europe. As a consequence, they endured the wrath of both royal reprisals and papal persecutions.

But these stalwart men stood undaunted and unintimidated. Out of those stormy waters a mighty ship hoisted its sails, setting a courageous course into virgin seas en route to a new world of freedom, hope, and truth.

Guiding this massive yet crippled vessel were strong, stubborn men: Luther, Calvin, Zwingli, Knox, Savonarola, Melanchthon, Hus, Tyndale, and Wycliffe.

Three flags flew over their ship—big, broad banners that announced their commitment, all of them taken from Scripture. These courageous men considered these principles so significant they were willing to die for them. And some did. The flags were:

NO SACRIFICE BUT CALVARY

NO PRIEST BUT CHRIST

NO CONFESSIONAL BUT THE THRONE OF GOD

These same emblazoned flags can be seen unfurled proudly over the book of Hebrews. And two of them can be seen waving over our verses for today's study.

## Our Goal: Resting in the Lord

For the first thirteen verses in chapter 4, the writer has been discussing the topic of rest. But his concept of rest is not to spread-eagle on the tropical coastline, basking in the Bahamian sun. To rest in the Lord means to relax in Him, to turn over to Him our worries and anxieties, to give Him the stress and strain of battle, and to enter into that resting place of relief. But how do we clutch out of overdrive and get smoothly in gear with God?

We obtain rest for our souls when we leave our churning with Him, when we enter into His presence with confidence, and when we wait for Him to work things out—all the while refusing to presume or panic or to let our pride get in the way.

## Our Need: Calling on the Lord

Hebrews 4:11 has stressed for us the importance of being diligent to enter God's rest. Verses 12–13 revealed where the Word fits in this process—showing us our real selves. As a climax to this section, we come to verse 14.

> Since then we have a great high priest who has passed through the heavens, Jesus the Son of God, let us hold fast our confession.

Regardless what the Word reveals in our life, there are two reasons why we shouldn't be hesitant to call for divine help: because we have a priest who is available, and because we have a confessional that is accessible. No sin is so great that it would turn the head of our high priest away from us. No sins are so numerous that they could bar the entrance to our confessional. Therefore, there is no reason why we should hesitate to come to Him in time of need.

But before we can confidently draw near to Jesus, there are a few questions we need answered.

One: *Who is this high priest?* Imagine the unique privilege of having as lobbyist for your cause the president's very own son. Talk about cutting through bureaucratic red tape and getting right to the top! That's exactly what we have with Jesus. He is no ordinary human priest but is the beloved Son of God, seated at the right hand of the Father, ever making intercession on our behalf (7:23–28).

Two: *What does this high priest have to offer?* Chapter 4, verses 15–16, refer to at least two: sympathy and grace.

> For we do not have a high priest who cannot sympathize with our weaknesses, but one who has been tempted in all things as we are, yet without sin. Let us therefore draw near with confidence to the throne of grace, that we may receive mercy and may find grace to help in time of need.

Our high priest sympathizes with our weakness (see Ps. 103:13–14). The Greek word for *sympathize* means "to suffer with." There's identification in that word. He has been tested as we are tested. He has known the searing sun and stinging sand of the wilderness. He has been weak as we are weak. He has suffered as we suffer. And He, too, has known what it's like to stand before the court and face its merciless judgment.

Besides sympathy, Jesus offers us grace. In fact, His throne is even called grace. Isn't that comforting? It's not called truth, justice, or the American way. Jesus doesn't sit in a courtroom, robed in condescension, scowling down from His bench to bring a gavel down on our lives as we stumble over our humiliating confessions. No, His throne is not a smug courtroom but a sympathetic confessional— a throne of grace.

Three: *Why does He qualify?* Jesus qualifies to be our high priest because, being the Son of God, He perfectly represents God (Heb. 4:14). At the same time, being fully man, Jesus perfectly represents humanity (v. 15). And finally, He qualifies because He is appointed by God to offer sacrifices for the sins of the people (Heb. 5:1–3 and 7:26–28).

Some people have the mistaken idea that once Jesus finished His work on the cross, He went to heaven to retire. Nothing could be farther from the truth. He lives to make intercession for us (Heb. 7:25, 9:24). As our high priest, He stands ready to hear our pleas, our petitions, and our pain. His ear is eager. His heart is empathetic. His hand is extended.

Over 250 years ago, the prolifically lyrical pen of Charles Wesley inked this hymn:

> Arise, my soul, arise!
> Shake off thy guilty fears;
> The bleeding Sacrifice
> In my behalf appears.
> Before the throne my Surety stands;
> My name is written on His hands,
> My name is written on His hands.
>
> He ever lives above,
> For me to intercede;
> His all-redeeming love,
> His precious blood to plead;
> His blood atoned for all our race,
> And sprinkles now the throne of grace,
> And sprinkles now the throne of grace. . . .

My God is reconciled,
His pardoning voice I hear;
He owns me for His child,
I can no longer fear:
With confidence I now draw nigh,
And "Father, Abba, Father!" cry,
And "Father, Abba, Father" cry.[1]

The fourth and final question we need answered before we will have this confidence to "draw nigh" is: *How does He provide?* The answer is found in 4:16. He provides by inviting us to draw near to Him with the promise that mercy and grace are in the divine hands He extends to us. Because of the King's invitation and the royal promise He offers, we can step up on the dais to His throne without groveling and without tedious ecclesiastical protocol. He bids us simply to come—confidently—without self-abasing pomp and pageantry.

## Our Hope: Responding to the Lord

The best example of this bidding by the Savior is found in Matthew 11:28: "Come to Me, all who are weary and heavy-laden, and I will give you rest."

But how do we do that? How do we lay our worries and our woes at His feet and obtain His rest in return?

Remember the three banners flapping in the introduction? They will lead us to that place of rest. Resting requires that we approach God. To do that we need a sacrifice. And the flag the Reformation rallied around tells us that there is . . .

NO SACRIFICE BUT CALVARY

But approaching God means that we must be clean and forgiven. How do we obtain that cleansing and forgiveness? Through the intercessory work of a high priest. And who is that priest? Again, the flag signals us that there is . . .

NO PRIEST BUT CHRIST

But being clean calls for a full confession. Where do we go to make that confession? As we turn our eyes skyward again, we see the third flag, waving in the lofty breeze to inform us that there is . . .

NO CONFESSIONAL BUT THE THRONE OF GRACE

1. "Arise, My Soul, Arise!"

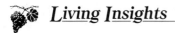 

We've been referring to Jesus as our high priest, but this term probably held much more meaning for the audience of Hebrews than it does for most of us today. Let's explore a passage that will deepen your understanding of this title.

- Exodus 28 describes the details of the priestly garments that Aaron wore. It's a topic that might appear inconsequential, but each article of clothing had a special significance, and learning about them rounds out the meaning of the title High Priest, which we sometimes use for Jesus. In the chart below, jot down your observations about each garment described in the passage and what it tells you about the Savior.

| Garment | Verse | Observation |
|---------|-------|-------------|
|         |       |             |

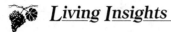 *Living Insights*

How often have you felt shut off from God, unworthy of His love, undeserving of His forgiveness? Take a few minutes to read Hebrews 3–10. As you read, circle the words *priest, high priest, priesthood,* and *great priest* every time they occur—you'll find over thirty references in those chapters.

- In what way does the priesthood of Christ affect your view of how God wants to relate to you?

_____

_____

_____

_____

_____

- How might this new understanding change the way you relate to Him?

_____

_____

_____

_____

_____

## Chapter 12

# GOD'S SON—OUR PRIEST
### Hebrews 5:1–10

The lights glare down on Dodger Stadium as "Take Me Out to the Ball Game" pipes over the public address system. Vendors hawk their wares, calling out, "Buttered popcorn, hot roasted peanuts!" All the while, every eye is transfixed on a blur of white that streaks from pitcher to catcher.

"Steeee-riiike three! You're out!" And the padded man in black behind the plate thumbs another batter to the dugout.

The umpire. Nobody on the field is as important as he is. Not the pitcher. Not the catcher. Not the batter. Not even the team's manager. For the umpire has the authority to make the final decisions that determine the outcome of the game. The umpire can decide whether to send a batter to first base or to the dugout. He can decide whether a sliding base runner is safe or out. He can throw out an unruly manager who kicks dirt at him or call off the game completely because of the weather.

As Job lamented about how the game of life was going against him, he yearned for someone standing behind the plate to make accurate calls about the curve balls that were coming his way.

"For He is not a man as I am that I may answer Him,
That we may go to court together.
There is no umpire between us,
Who may lay his hand upon us both." (Job 9:32–33)

Job speaks for all of us. We all need an umpire who will mediate between us and God.

## The Universal Priesthood of the Believer

The great announcement in Hebrews 4–5 is that we now have an umpire. The One for whom Job searched, we have found.

For there is one God, and one mediator also between
God and men, the man Christ Jesus. (1 Tim. 2:5)

Regardless whether the people in the nickel seats boo our lives, if Jesus calls us "safe," we're safe. That's all that counts. His judgment is what matters—not the catcalls from the crowd. For His judgment stands long after the bleachers have emptied and the lights in the ballpark have been turned off.

But this umpire not only mediates between God and us, He also intercedes on our behalf, continually, as our high priest. In fact, one of the greatest changes Jesus Christ made in the lives of believers was to eliminate our need for some other human priest to represent us to God. Now, because of Christ, we can go to God on our own. As believer-priests we can bring God our own needs, our own sins, our own requests. And Jesus, who sits at the right hand of the Father, hears those prayers and represents us to Him.

## The Earthly Priests of the Jews

From sandlot games to baseball cards to shirtsleeve Saturday afternoons at the ballpark, twentieth-century kids have grown up on baseball. And just as those kids are familiar with every star and statistic of the game, so the first-century Jews were familiar with the sacrificial system. They talked about priests, animals, blood, and altars in the same familiar way many people today talk about baseball. And it is such a conversation that we come upon in Hebrews 5.

> For every high priest taken from among men is appointed on behalf of men in things pertaining to God, in order to offer both gifts and sacrifices for sins; he can deal gently with the ignorant and misguided, since he himself also is beset with weakness; and because of it he is obligated to offer sacrifices for sins, as for the people, so also for himself. And no one takes the honor to himself, but receives it when he is called by God, even as Aaron was. (vv. 1–4)

The writer lists three simple, yet serious, qualifications for a priest. First, he must represent God (vv. 1–2). Second, he must offer sacrifices for sin (v. 3). And third, he must be called by God; he cannot be self-appointed (v. 4).

The priest functioned as a spiritual umpire for the Jewish people. He had the discerning eye that could judge between right and wrong and answer to God on the people's behalf.

In the second half of verse 4 an example of a priest is given—Aaron. His ordination into the priesthood is recorded in Exodus 28.

> "Then bring near to yourself Aaron your brother, and his sons with him, from among the sons of Israel, to minister as priest to Me—Aaron, Nadab and Abihu, Eleazar and Ithamar, Aaron's sons. And you shall make

holy garments for Aaron your brother, for glory and for beauty. And you shall speak to all the skillful persons whom I have endowed with the spirit of wisdom, that they make Aaron's garments to consecrate him, that he may minister as priest to Me. . . . And they shall be on Aaron and on his sons when they enter the tent of meeting, or when they approach the altar to minister in the holy place, so that they do not incur guilt and die. It shall be a statute forever to him and to his descendants after him." (vv. 1–3, 43)

Being a priest was serious business with strict rules—even the details of the priestly garments' design were divinely ordained. And if those rules were disobeyed, a priest could lose his life.

## The Heavenly Priest of the Throne

Regardless of how sacred the priesthood was, God never intended it to be a permanent institution, especially after the supreme sacrifice was made—the sacrifice of His Son. In place of the human priesthood God ordained Jesus as a heavenly priest.

So also Christ did not glorify Himself so as to become a high priest, but He who said to Him,
"Thou art My Son,
Today I have begotten Thee"; . . .
In the days of His flesh, He offered up both prayers and supplications with loud crying and tears to the One able to save Him from death, and He was heard because of His piety. Although He was a Son, He learned obedience from the things which He suffered. And having been made perfect, He became to all those who obey Him the source of eternal salvation. (Heb. 5:5, 7–9)

See the words, "So also Christ . . ."? They make a comparison with Aaron's priestly call, mentioned in verse 4. And in doing so, they show that Jesus is superior as a high priest—even to Aaron. Aaron was appointed by God from the tribe of Levi, while Jesus is the Incarnate God who is one with the Father (v. 5). Aaron, who offered many sacrifices, was himself a sinner, while Jesus is perfect and "a priest forever" (vv. 6, 9). Aaron provided temporal assistance, while Jesus provides eternal salvation once for all (v. 9).

Jesus is not one among many priests; He is the final priest. He was not one among many sacrifices; He was the final sacrifice. He was not self-appointed; He was God-appointed. He wasn't distant and cold; He was a man like us who offered up prayers and sacrifices. He is not a superhuman robot; He is truly one who represents us to God.

In verses 6 and 10, the order of Christ's priesthood is designated.

> Just as He says also in another passage,
> "Thou art a priest forever
> According to the order of
> Melchizedek." . . .
> being designated by God as a high priest according to
> the order of Melchizedek.

We will discuss the order of Melchizedek in greater detail when we get to Hebrews 7, but for now we just want to give a brief, baseball card biography of his life.

First, Melchizedek was a man who lived in the days of Abraham. He was both a king and a priest. The salient point here is that Aaron was only a priest. Throughout the Old Testament no one but Melchizedek appeared in this dual role. Similarly, Jesus is both a King and a priest (see Psalm 110).

Second, Melchizedek appears all alone. There is no mention of his parentage or his lineage. The implication is that he did not inherit his priesthood. Mysteriously he appears, serves, speaks, and then disappears from the scene. Similarly, Jesus comes on the scene "like a tender shoot, And like a root out of parched ground. . . . A man of sorrows, and acquainted with grief" (Isa. 53:2, 3).

Third, Melchizedek did not pass his priesthood on to a successor. The order of Melchizedek was a priestly order of one person only. There wasn't a monastery of Melchizedekian priests sequestered away somewhere in Salem. Similarly, the priesthood of Jesus is unique. There is no succession of the mantle that God laid on his shoulders. He wears it to this day, and he wears it like no other could. He stands as the unique umpire of all time.

## The Application of the Priesthood of Christ

The subject of the priesthood is not all ancient history and dry doctrine. There is much we can apply that addresses the needs we have today.

First, we need a priest who isn't prejudiced, who doesn't discriminate between male or female, slave or free, Greek or Jew—an unbiased representative who can accurately represent our case, not one who will pad the record or misrepresent our situation. And we have such a priest in Jesus.

Second, we need a permanent priest to stand before the presence of God. We need full-time help, not somebody who works nine to five with weekends off. That way we know we're safe twenty-four hours a day, every day. And we have such a priest in Jesus.

Third, we need the assurance of knowing we are safe in the presence of God. We need a heavenly umpire that calls 'em as He sees 'em. An umpire that calls a ball, a ball, and a strike, a strike. An umpire that doesn't waver when the fans boo. That way, when He says we're safe, we have the confidence that we are. And we have that assurance in Jesus.

Aren't those wonderful thoughts? They give a real sense of security and rest, don't they? And that's exactly why the writer to the Hebrews included them—so we could face the game of life with confidence, even if we're up against a double header with the Giants.

 *Living Insights* STUDY ONE

In our lesson we learned that Jesus acts as our high priest, but did you know that you, as a believer in Christ, are a priest as well? In the Old Testament, the role of the priest was that of offering sacrifices to God for the people. What many of us have forgotten is that believers today are responsible for sacrifices also.

- As you read the three Bible verses below, look for the word *sacrifice*. Then, summarize the meaning of each particular act of sacrifice.

**The Believer-Priest and Sacrifice**

Romans 12:1

Summary: _____

_____

_____

Philippians 4:18

Summary: _____

_____

_____

Hebrews 13:16

Summary: _____

_____

_____

*Living Insights*

We were able to scratch the surface regarding the believer-priest
and the acts of sacrifice. It was a nice, neat little Bible study, but
what does it mean to you?

• This exercise looks a great deal like the preceding one, but there
  is one important change: this time, instead of summarizing each
  verse, write in some concrete and specific ways you can apply
  these verses to your life.

### The Believer-Priest and Sacrifice

Romans 12:1

Application: _____

_____

_____

Philippians 4:18

Application: _____

_____

_____

Hebrews 13:16

Application: _____

_____

_____

## Chapter 13

# LET'S GROW UP!

### Hebrews 5:11–14

Aw, grow up!" Ever hear those words? Maybe they were uttered in disgust by an older brother. Or spoken in jest by a friend. Or blurted in exasperation by one of your parents.

When you finally did grow up, you put away childish things, such as dumping a half pound of sugar on your cereal, throwing hissy fits when you didn't get your way, or chanting "Sticks and stones may break my bones, but words will never hurt me."

But, let's face it, we all act like children from time to time, don't we? Figuratively speaking, we all still throw an occasional block, bite back, spill our milk, and threaten to take our ball and go home.

The older we get, the harder it is to choke down the words "Aw, grow up." Especially when it comes to spiritual things. Yet some of us are still immature in that part of our lives. We still crawl around in our training pants, suck our thumbs, and cling to our security blankets.

Today, we're going to try to change all that. We're going to take a few baby steps to help strengthen our legs so we can get off the floor once and for all—and grow up.

### A Brief Analysis of Growth

Growth is something that's important to all of us. From the moment we're born, we're weighed and measured. Our growth is monitored by the pediatrician and later measured by our parents with marks on the wall that chart our progress with each passing year. However, our spiritual stature may be dwarfed when compared to the marks on our physical growth chart—for growth within does not always match growth without.

The Bible speaks a lot about spiritual growth:

> Brethren, do not be children in your thinking, . . . but in your thinking be mature. (1 Cor. 14:20)

> We are no longer to be children . . . we are to grow up. (Eph. 4:14–15)

> Like newborn babes, long for the pure milk of the
> word, that by it you may grow. (1 Pet. 2:2)

We come into God's family the same way we come into our physical family—by being born into it (John 3:1–8). And we grow spiritually much the same way we grow physically—by taking in nourishment and getting the right kind of exercise (1 Pet. 2:2, 1 Cor. 9:24–27). If we keep on growing, keep on exercising, and stay healthy, we will become spiritually mature (Eph. 4:11–16).

But there is no guarantee that this process will continue unimpeded. For though growth is the *natural* result of nutrition and exercise, it is not the *inevitable* result. More often than not, something stunts the growth. That's exactly what we find toward the end of Hebrews 5—a group of Christians old enough to be cutting their own meat but who were still eating baby food from a spoon.

## When Immaturity Is Prolonged

The scene in Hebrews 5 is a tragic one. It looks more like a day-care center than a church—grown men and women sitting around in circles playing with ABC blocks.[1] They ought to know better. They ought to grow up. But there they sit, playing in the nursery school of elemental truths.

> Concerning [Melchizedek] we have much to say, and it is hard to explain, since you have become dull of hearing. For though by this time you ought to be teachers, you have need again for someone to teach you the elementary principles of the oracles of God, and you have come to need milk and not solid food. For everyone who partakes only of milk is not accustomed to the word of righteousness, for he is a babe. But solid food is for the mature, who because of practice have their senses trained to discern good and evil. (vv. 11–14)

---

1. "The writer says that they still need someone to teach them *the simple elements* (*stoicheia*) *of Christianity.* This word has a variety of meanings. In grammar it means the letters of the alphabet, the A B C; in physics it means the four basic elements of which the world is composed; in geometry it means the elements of proof like the point and the straight line; in philosophy it means the first elementary principles with which the students begin. It is the sorrow of the writer to the Hebrews that after many years of Christianity his people have never got past the rudiments; they are like children who do not know the difference between right and wrong." William Barclay, *The Letter to the Hebrews,* rev. ed., The Daily Study Bible Series (Philadelphia, Pa.: Westminster Press, 1976), p. 50.

### What We Become

Admittedly, the preceding discussion about Melchizedek and the priesthood of Christ was a complex one (5:1–10). But these Hebrew Christians had cut their theological teeth a long time ago. Surely by now they were able to bite off something as meaty as this. But they weren't. Why? Because of what they had become—"dull of hearing" (v. 11).

The Greek word for "dull" is used only here and in 6:12 in the entire New Testament.[2] It means "thick, slow, sluggish, indolent, lazy." Interestingly, the original term is from two words, meaning "no" and "push." A dull speaker, for instance, would be one with "no push," whose get-up-and-go got up and went. But seldom do we apply the word to the audience. Seldom do we accuse them of being dull listeners. But that was the condition of this Hebrew audience.

When immaturity is prolonged, this is what we become—insensitive, uncaring, and unresponsive. In a word, dull.

### Why It Happens

First: *We become dull because we fail to grow up as we grow older.* Age alone does not produce maturity. Wrinkles? Yes. Senility? Sometimes. But maturity? No. Marking time is not the same as marching forward, "for those who are older are said to be wiser; but it is not mere age that makes men wise" (Job 32:7–8).[3]

Second: *We become dull because our poor habits prevent healthy development.* Look carefully at the spiritual habits cultivated by the Hebrews. They had a habit of taking in food, but not giving it out to others (Heb. 5:12a). They had become accustomed to being babies. They liked the cuddly comforts of the crib. And they liked to partake of a diet that consisted just of milk—not only was it sweet, but it went down smoothly and was digested easily (vv. 12b–13).[4]

---

2. The word is *nōthros*. In the Septuagint, the Greek translation of the Old Testament, it is found in Proverbs 22:29, where it is translated "obscure men" in contrast to "kings." Christians who are "dull of hearing" lead lives of obscurity and fail to impact the lives of others or the culture around them.

3. The Living Bible (Wheaton, Ill.: Tyndale House Publishers, 1971).

4. In verse 13 the phrase "not accustomed to the word of righteousness" characterizes the babe in Christ. Interestingly, the words *not accustomed* mean "without trial" or "without experience of" and have the sense of meaning "unskilled." Just as a baby is unskilled when it comes to cutting a thick steak placed on its high chair, so these Christians didn't quite know what to do with the meatier things of God.

### True Marks of Maturity

Babies desire to be fed, burped, changed, and entertained. But God has a better plan for His children than toddling about in the nursery. His plan is that we grow up, that we mature. Three marks of maturity are found in verse 14.

> But solid food is for the mature, who because of practice have their senses trained to discern good and evil.

#### Good Food

"Solid food" is something you can sink your teeth into. It's not formula warmed to body temperature and bottle-fed; it's something that takes work and preparation and time. It's not something to pacify your palate; it's substance to produce a strong body.

#### The Right Kind of Activity

"Practice" is what it takes to accurately apply the Word to our life. Practice, practice, practice. Hour after hour. Day after day. Year after year. We can't expect to be suckled on Sunday morning and not have another feeding for a week. We have to convert the food we take in and put it to use. And we have to do this day in and day out.

#### Keen Senses

"Senses trained to discern good and evil" are another mark of maturity. We need to develop highly sensitive antennae to distinguish between the helpful and the harmful information we're exposed to on a daily basis. We need to have our feelers out, constantly testing the world around us and recoiling from any doctrine that is foreign to the Scriptures and harmful if swallowed.

### A Practical Training Program

Just as we need to take in the right kind of food, so we also need to take in a variety of food. We need a balanced diet. We don't need an all-grapefruit diet or an all-protein diet or an all-carbohydrate diet. We need food from all four food groups.

The same dietary principles hold true in the spiritual realm. We shouldn't look to one teacher as our sole source of nourishment. We should have a balanced diet of teaching from a number of different people. That way, we won't be so prone to fall off the deep end spiritually or get involved in personality worship or some other cult experience.

Remember, to achieve healthy growth we need three things: nourishing food, sufficient exercise, and keen discernment.

We need to avoid junk food and stick with a diet organically grown from Scripture. We need to learn to prepare it ourselves as opposed to settling for some attractively packaged TV dinner. And finally, we need to chew our food slowly and digest it thoroughly. There are a lot of spiritual bulimics who binge on Sunday and purge on Monday morning. We can't expect to grow up healthy with poor eating habits.

Next, we need sufficient and sustained exercise. And we need to make it tough enough to work up a sweat. No pain, no gain! We need Bible study that challenges us. We need relationships that spur us on and keep us on the right track.

Then, we need to hone a keen edge on our ability to discern truth from error. We need to be able to cut through the fat and get to the meat of a person's teaching. We need to be able to spot a good steak from a pound of baloney. And there's a lot of baloney on the religious market these days.

Finally, we need to remember that although growth is a natural process, it isn't an inevitable one.

 **_Living Insights_**

Hebrews 5:14 presents a very practical training program for staying healthy. Three essentials are covered: nourishing food, sufficent exercise, and keen discernment. Interestingly, the book of James develops these same topics. Look up the passages listed below, and write out your observations regarding these essentials.

### Nourishing Food (James 1:19–25)

_____

_____

_____

_____

_____

_____

## Sufficient Exercise (James 2:14–26)

_____

_____

_____

_____

_____

## Keen Discernment (James 3:13–18)

_____

_____

_____

_____

_____

### Living Insights                          STUDY TWO

Now that we've become familiar with the three essentials of staying healthy, let's turn our attention to incorporating them into our lives. Answer each question below honestly and thoughtfully.

• How would I describe my intake of nourishing "food"?

_____

_____

_____

_____

_____

94

- How would I describe my exercise program for applying the Word?

_____

_____

_____

_____

_____

_____

- What evidences in my life show I am a person with keen discernment?

_____

_____

_____

_____

_____

_____

## Chapter 14

# THE PERIL OF
# FALLING AWAY
*Hebrews 6:1–8*

Hebrews 6 is the Rubik's Cube of the Bible. No matter how you twist and turn the individual verses, they don't seem to quite fit within the neatly fixed corners of our theological framework.

But just as Rubik's Cube has a solution, so does the frustrating puzzle of Hebrews 6. It takes hands that are both skillful and patient to solve the mystery, but it can be done. And it can be done in such a way as to square with the rest of Scripture.

So limber up your mental fingers and get ready to take apart this exegetical enigma, verse by verse.

## Going Back: A Few Reminders

In our last study we looked at Hebrews 5:11–14. The subject of those verses was Christian maturity, something the author's readers were stunted in, as Philip Edgcumbe Hughes notes.

> One who is so unadvanced that he needs to be introduced once more to the ABCs of the faith is no better than a child in spiritual understanding: *milk* is the only diet suited to his immature condition, *not* the *solid food* of sound Christian doctrine. To go on living on milk, mere baby-food, is indicative of arrested development, and the recipients of this letter have evidently failed to advance beyond, or have relapsed into, a state of spiritual infancy. Instead of being strong and well developed, they are weaklings in the faith.[1]

The last paragraph of Hebrews 5 delineates three essentials for spiritual growth.

1. Solid food—meat, not just milk.

2. Consistent practice—putting the truth into action.

1. Philip Edgcumbe Hughes, *A Commentary on the Epistle to the Hebrews* (Grand Rapids, Mich.: William B. Eerdmans Publishing Co., 1977), pp. 190–91.

3. Keen discernment—the ability to judge between good and evil.

Take away any one of these basic building blocks and growth can be radically impaired.

## Pressing On: A Continual Objective

A major goal for the Christian is growing up—not just growing older, not just marking time till eternity, not just dwelling on the basics.

> Therefore leaving the elementary teaching about the Christ, let us press on to maturity, not laying again a foundation of repentance from dead works and of faith toward God, of instruction about washings, and laying on of hands, and the resurrection of the dead, and eternal judgment. (6:1–2)

Instead of pressing on to maturity, the Hebrews have been toddling around the kindergarten of Christian truth, glancing through their "see-Spot-run" readers when they should have been studying Shakespeare.[2]

To get specific, the writer lists three categories of truths that belong on the bottom shelf of primers: *conversion*—"not laying again a foundation of repentance from dead works and of faith toward God;" *church policy and preferences*—"instructions about washings, and laying on of hands;" and *prophecy*—"the resurrection of the dead, and eternal judgment."

The truth about conversion is foundational to the Christian life. But once the foundation is in place, we need to press on to complete the rest of the building. We need to concentrate on the walls to give it support, on the siding to keep out the wind, and on the roof to provide shelter from the rain. Similarly, the debate about modes of baptism and methods of ecclesiastical ritual is important, but it pales by comparison to the more crucial areas of the Christian life. As does the chronology of future events. For regardless of how essential all this information is, it is elementary. And after years in the

---

2. "The writer to the Hebrews says that his people must be going on to what he calls *teleiotēs*. . . . Pythagoras divided his students into *hoi manthanontes, the learners,* and *hoi teleioi, the mature.* Philo divided his students into three different classes—*hoi archomenoi, those just beginning, hoi prokoptontes, those making progress,* and *hoi teleiōmenoi, those beginning to reach maturity."* William Barclay, *The Letter to the Hebrews,* rev. ed., The Daily Study Bible Series (Philadelphia, Pa.: Westminster Press, 1976), p. 52.

faith, we want to grow up and get on with our education—not end up as college-age Christians still toying with grade school curriculum.

If you're hung up on prophecy, you're not going on in the faith. If you're hung up on some mode of baptism, you're not graduating to higher levels in the Christian life. If you're hung up on the gospel and nothing more, you're not growing. If you're at one of those impasses in your walk with God, you're jogging in place. You may be getting a lot of exercise, but you're going nowhere. The writer's advice to you is "press on to maturity."

And this we shall do, if God permits. (v. 3)

*If.* The condition is crucial. "If God permits." He stands at the doors of our spiritual education as the principal who determines whether we matriculate or graduate, whether we pass or fail, whether we move on to the next grade or are held back a year. He holds the keys—He, and He alone.

## Falling Away: A Dangerous Peril

Verse 3 is a transition that leads to the writer's next point. In verses 1–2, he states that the major goal for the Christian is growing up. Now he discusses the major problem that would prevent us from accomplishing that goal—falling away.

> For in the case of those who have once been en-lightened and have tasted of the heavenly gift and have been made partakers of the Holy Spirit, and have tasted the good word of God and the powers of the age to come, and then have fallen away, it is impossible to renew them again to repentance, since they again crucify to themselves the Son of God, and put Him to open shame. For ground that drinks the rain which often falls upon it and brings forth vegetation useful to those for whose sake it is also tilled, receives a blessing from God; but if it yields thorns and thistles, it is worthless and close to being cursed, and it ends up being burned. (vv. 4–8)

Notice that the ground remains intact, but it is burned so as to consume the worthless vegetation it has produced. Those who fall away are not burned up. Rather, the barren branches are what come under the scorching flame at the Judgment Seat of Christ.[3] When

---

3. Compare 1 Corinthians 3:10–15, 9:24–27, 1 Timothy 1:18–20, 2 Timothy 4:9–10, 14–15.

we translate the cacophony of commentators on these verses, the interpretations fall into two main positions.

1. *The people referred to in the passage are saved.* They have been enlightened. They have tasted of the heavenly gift. They have partaken of the Holy Spirit. They have tasted the Word of God and the powers of the age to come. Consequently, the falling away in verse 6 means they have lost their salvation.

2. *The people referred to in the passage are unsaved.* These people profess but do not possess new life in Christ. They are enlightened but not on fire with the truth. They've tasted the heavenly gift but not digested it. They've become partakers of the Spirit but not possessors of Him. They have sampled the Word but not savored it. They have had a brush with the supernatural but not a born-again experience.

If position number one is correct, after backsliding there is no way the person can ever be saved again. Verse 6 says it's *impossible*—not difficult—for that person to be renewed to repentance.

If position number two is correct, the author has used the same set of terms but with two different meanings. For he uses the same terms to describe the born-again state as he does the unregenerate state.[4]

So, what do we do with this Rubik's Cube? Put it back on the coffee table and give up? No. We just need to collect our thoughts and apply a little common sense.

As we step back from this enigmatic passage, the context becomes a critical clue to its solution. The book of Hebrews was written to people who had been born into the family of God. And the admonition to "press on to maturity" logically would be addressed to children within that family—not those outside. Also, the terms "enlightened . . . tasted of the heavenly gift . . . partakers of the Holy Spirit . . . tasted the good word of God" are all labels we would most likely use to describe Christians, not non-Christians.

The next step in unlocking the mystery of these verses takes us to the terms *repentance* (v. 6) and *vegetation* (v. 7). The passage does not speak about salvation of the unsaved but about the repentance of the saved; it doesn't speak to the issue of corrupt roots but of worthless fruit.

---

4. Compare his use of "enlightened" in Hebrews 6:4 with that in 10:32, and "tasted . . . the powers of the age to come" in 6:5 with 2:4.

Instead of abiding in Christ, the true vine, and producing fruit, those who sever themselves from His influence wither away in insignificant labor (John 15:1–6). Their deeds provide neither beauty nor shade nor sustenance for others. They are, in a word, useless. And these corrupt deeds are good for nothing except to be burned in the trash pile.[5]

The actual peril spoken of in the passage is that believers can pull so far away from their spiritual moorings that they become hopelessly adrift on a sea of carnality. This ship of fools can live it up on a floating den of iniquity and sail so far off course that God may refuse them passage back to the harbor of rest. A terrifying possibility when you think about it. Even more terrifying when the person drifting is someone you love.

## Looking Within: A Needed Examination

First Corinthians 10:12 issues a sobering warning: "Let him who thinks he stands take heed lest he fall." No matter how closely we walk with God, we need to realize that every step is the beginning of a fall. Every mountaintop experience is bounded by steep chasms into which we could take a precipitous tumble.

Take a minute to examine where you stand. Is the theological rock you're standing on a little shaky? Is there a chasm of carnality only a few steps from where you're standing? Are you toying with the idea of taking a plunge into that chasm? If so, now is the time to take heed to the warning in Hebrews 6. For who knows how far you can go before God refuses you the opportunity for a renewal that will lead to your repentance.

---

5. " 'If they fall away' means 'fall away from Christianity.' The verb *parapiptō* is found only here in the NT, and its meaning is clear. The writer is envisaging people who have been numbered among the followers of Christ but now leave that company. Such cannot be brought back to repentance. Notice that he does not say 'cannot be forgiven' or 'cannot be restored to salvation' or the like. It is repentance that is in mind, and the writer says that it is impossible for these people to repent. . . . There is no putting the clock back. But it seems more likely that the reference is to a repentance that means leaving the backsliding into which the person has fallen. He cannot bring himself to this repentance." Leon Morris, "Hebrews," *The Expositor's Bible Commentary,* gen. ed. Frank E. Gaebelein (Grand Rapids, Mich.: Zondervan Publishing House, 1981), vol. 12, p. 55.

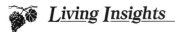 **_Living Insights_** STUDY ONE

Examine yourself in light of the illustrations used in Hebrews 6.

> For ground that drinks the rain which often falls upon
> it and brings forth vegetation useful to those for whose
> sake it is also tilled, receives a blessing from God. (v. 7)

> But if it yields thorns and thistles, it is worthless and
> close to being cursed, and it ends up being burned. (v. 8)

Describe a time in your life that paralleled the picture in verse 7.

_____

_____

_____

_____

_____

Describe a time in your life that paralleled verse 8.

_____

_____

_____

_____

_____

What was it that brought you to repent and to return to God?

_____

_____

_____

_____

_____

Take a few minutes to reflect on God's work in bringing you
back, and pray in appreciation for your safe return.

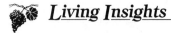 *Living Insights*
STUDY TWO

After a message as sobering as this one, we have an all-important task to carry out. It is the task of examining ourselves.

- Let's just spend our time thinking in silence. While reflecting, think about some hard questions. Pray through each question and ask God's Spirit to reveal the answers to you as you pray.

  —Am I flirting with the peril of falling away?

  —Have I begun to drift dangerously near the point of no return?

  —As a child of God, what is needed to keep me walking near the Savior?

  —Are there more thorns than fruit being produced in my life?

  —What exactly is God's warning to me right now?

  Now take the time to go through what God has revealed to you, and pray for repentance for any areas where you are falling short.

## Chapter 15

# THE BRIGHTER SIDE

*Hebrews 6:9–12*

Affirmation . . . a little goes a long way. In fact, a pat on the back gets far greater motivational mileage than a kick in the pants, as these findings from a second-grade classroom illustrate.

Two psychologists spent several days at the back of the room with stopwatches, carefully observing the behavior of both the children and the teacher. Every 10 seconds they recorded on their pads how many children were out of their seats. On the average, some child was standing 360 times in every 20-minute period and the teacher said "Sit down!" 7 times in every 20-minute period.

The psychologists suggested that she consciously increase the number of times she commanded "Sit down!" and see what would happen. So in the next few days, according to the observers, she yelled "Sit down!" an average of 27.5 times per 20-minute period. Did that change the children's behavior? Indeed it did. They were out of their seats 540 times per period, or *an increase of 50%.* To check their data, the researchers asked the teacher to return to her normal number of reprimands and the level of roaming declined to exactly the normal rate within two days. Then for another two days the "Sit down!" commands were increased, and sure enough, the number of children out of their seats increased again.

Here is the kicker. For the final week, the researchers asked that the teacher refrain entirely from yelling "Sit down!" and instead quietly compliment children who were staying in their seats doing their work. The result? *The roaming about decreased by 33%, the best behavior for the entire experiment.*[1]

---

1. Alan Loy McGinnis, *The Friendship Factor* (Minneapolis, Minn.: Augsburg Publishing House, 1979), pp. 93–94.

The incident illustrates Goethe's remarks: "Correction does much, but encouragement does more."[2] That famous German writer went on to say that "encouragement after censure is as the sun after a shower."[3] In our study of Hebrews, the first eight verses of chapter 6 came upon us suddenly and inclemently, like a torrential downpour. However, verses 9–12 pierce through the clouds with shafts of encouragement to dry us off and chase away the chills.

Today we want to focus on the brighter side and bask in the sunshine of affirmation.

## The End of a Negative Warning

Before we step into that dazzling sunshine, however, let's take a step back into the dripping rain of verses 1–8. The strong command in verses 1–3 is to "press on to maturity," or to use the modern vernacular, to "grow up." If we don't, we face a grim consequence. If we refuse to grow up and stubbornly decide to sit in the playpen, we will be vulnerable to the debilitating diseases of the heart, without a spiritually mature immune system to ward off the deadly infections so prevalent all around us. And once infected, our growth may become stunted and we may never recover to go on to maturity.

## The Encouragement of Positive Assurance

The extreme warning in verses 1–8 undoubtedly had explosive results in the lives of its readers. But blasting is often necessary before building can begin. Now with the rubble cleared away, the writer begins some constructive affirmation.

> But, beloved, we are convinced of better things concerning you, and things that accompany salvation, though we are speaking in this way. (v. 9)

"But . . ." In contrast to the judgment that would befall the moral and theological apostates mentioned in verses 4–8, the writer sees a different future for his readers. The writer doesn't call them knuckleheads or losers; he calls them "beloved." Isn't that wonderful? Isn't that the way you'd like to be treated when you've dropped the ball somewhere or failed to measure up in some circumstance?

There's something tremendously affirming about hearing reassuring words from someone you respect. So often the dignity of self-

2. *The New Dictionary of Thoughts*, comp. Tyron Edwards, rev. and enl. by C. N. Catrevas, Jonathan Edwards, and Ralph Emerson Browns (Standard Book Co., 1966), p. 172.

3. *The New Dictionary of Thoughts*, p. 172.

respect hangs from the fragile thread of other people's confidence in us, others' assurance that we are trustworthy.

Question: How could the writer have such a high opinion of his readers? The reason for his confidence is found in verse 10.

> For God is not unjust so as to forget your work and the love which you have shown toward His name, in having ministered and in still ministering to the saints.

The writer is confident of better things for his readers' lives because they have already demonstrated the good fruit of serving others and are continuing to do so—none of which has escaped God's watchful eye. The writer's ultimate confidence is in the justice of God. A just God could not overlook a single good work done on His behalf, nor could He overlook the motivation of the heart—love (compare Matt. 6:2–6 with Acts 10:1–4). It's interesting to note that the writer mentions both an appreciation for their work and for their attitudes.

*Appreciation.* It's what we all live for, and it's what some even die for. American psychologist William James noted: "The deepest principle in human nature is the craving to be appreciated."[4] Not needing. Not hoping. Not desiring. But "craving." Within the deepest catacombs of our heart, a cry echoes—a cry to be appreciated.

You may not be appreciated by those around you, but you can show others your appreciation for them. You can give them a smile, a kind word, a pat on the back, a thank-you note. As Proverbs 3:27 exhorts us:

> Do not withhold good from those to whom it is due,
> When it is in your power to do it.

Today, try being a little more generous in giving praise to those around you. Try a little tenderness. Try showing appreciation unto others as you would have appreciation shown unto you. And if you do, Proverbs has a really great promise you can look forward to:

> There is one who scatters, yet increases all the more,
> And there is one who withholds what is justly due,
>     but it results only in want.
> The generous man will be prosperous,
> And he who waters will himself be watered.
> (11:24–25)

4. William James, as quoted in *Topical Encyclopedia of Living Quotations*, ed. Sherwood Eliot Wirt and Kersten Beckstrom (Minneapolis, Minn.: Bethany House Publishers, 1982), p. 9.

Little by little, that smile, that kind word, that pat on the back, that note of appreciation will find their way back to you.

In Hebrews 6:11–12 the writer adds a footnote of clarification.

> And we desire that each one of you show the same diligence so as to realize the full assurance of hope until the end, that you may not be sluggish, but imitators of those who through faith and patience inherit the promises.

In these two verses, the writer encapsulates three exhortations. He specifies his desire—"show the same diligence." He reminds them of the danger—"that you may not be sluggish." And he motivates them to stand firm—"but [be] imitators of those who through faith and patience inherit the promises."

Between the lines of these exhortations we can find how to "press on to maturity" to reach our full potential. Negatively, we must be diligent to fight laziness. Positively, we must have models to follow. The former motivation is intrinsic, coming from within; the latter is extrinsic, coming from without.

But even in the absence of role models or affirmation, the responsibility for pressing on to maturity rests squarely on our own shoulders. When we stand before the Judgment Seat of Christ, we won't be able to point a finger of blame at anyone else but ourselves (2 Cor. 5:10). God didn't accept that from Adam when he palmed off the blame on Eve (Gen. 3:12)—nor will He from us.

## On Becoming People Who Affirm Others

If you struggle with showing affirmation and appreciation to others, here are three hints that should be of some help.

First: *Stop limiting your comments to the weaknesses of others.* To be sure, there are times we have to blast before we can build. But our goal is to build up—not to tear down (1 Cor. 3:10, Eph. 4:11–13).

Second: *Start focusing on the strengths of others.* Find what's solid in a person's life and build on that with encouragement (Heb. 10:24–25).

Third: *Forget the darker side of others and remember the brighter side.* Certainly every person, like every moon, has a dark side. But our appreciation for others is enhanced by focusing on their bright side—not on the craters in the shadowy side of their character.[5]

5. For an excellent study on this whole subject of affirmation, read *The Blessing* (Nashville, Tenn.: Thomas Nelson Publishers, 1986) and *The Gift of Honor* (Nashville, Tenn.: Thomas Nelson Publishers, 1987), both by Gary Smalley and John Trent, Ph.D.

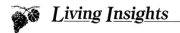 **Living Insights**

The first twelve verses of Hebrews 6 show a stark contrast in tone—we see within them a negative warning and a positive affirmation. Take a look at the verses again to better understand the correlation between them.

- As you reread these twelve verses, look for two types of statements: warning and affirmation. Briefly jot the statements in the following charts.

| Warnings | |
|---|---|
| Verse | Statement |
|  |  |

| Affirmations | |
|---|---|
| Verse | Statement |
|  |  |

- Which of the statements you found are most applicable to you at this point in your life? Place a check beside each one that seems relevant.

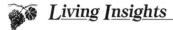 *Living Insights*

We should all strive to be like the writer to the Hebrews—maintaining an equilibrium between warning and encouragement. But for most of us, criticism comes far more readily to our tongues than praise.

Are you a person who is known for encouragement and affirmation? Think now—when was the last time you knowingly set out to be an encouragement to someone?

- This is your assignment: Be an encouragment! You figure out the specifics. Think of someone you would like to encourage or who you think needs your encouragement. Then plan a very special way in which to do just that. It may be a visit, a note, an inexpensive gift, a phone call, a hug, or all of the above! It really doesn't matter, as long as it's from your heart.

Chapter 16

# HOPE FOR THOSE WHO DOUBT

*Hebrews 6:13–20*

Doubts are question marks in our theology that can painfully punctuate our prayers. But no matter how bewildering the pain, doubts serve the purpose of drawing us closer to God, as the following quote indicates:

> "Those who believe they believe in God, but without passion in the heart, without anguish of mind, without uncertainty, without doubt, and even at times without despair, believe only in the idea of God, and not in God himself."[1]

Doubt is a precursor to faith. Just as we come to God through faith, we come to faith through doubt. Doubt brings us to the throne of God so that we can have a hearing with the King of the universe to get our questions answered. Sometimes we come despondent. Sometimes we come defiant. But regardless of how we come, doubt brings us there. And for that we should be thankful.

In today's study we want to offer hope for those who doubt, by looking at the life of Abraham.

## Doubts Increase

There are times when doubts run amuck in our lives. And they seem to run most rampant in three situations.

### When things I believe should never happen, happen.

As Christians we trust in a God who is good and just and gracious and loving and merciful. But there are times in life when He seems just the opposite. Times when things happen that don't seem to fit with the character of God. When things happen that don't come out in the theological wash. When bad things happen to good people, as Rabbi Harold Kushner writes:

> There is only one question which really matters:
> why do bad things happen to good people? All other

1. Unamuno, as quoted by Madeleine L'Engle, in *Walking on Water: Reflections on Faith and Art* (Wheaton, Ill.: Harold Shaw Publishers, 1980), p. 32.

theological conversation is intellectually diverting; somewhat like doing the crossword puzzle in the Sunday paper and feeling very satisfied when you have made the words fit; but ultimately without the capacity to reach people where they really care. Virtually every meaningful conversation I have ever had with people on the subject of God and religion has either started with this question, or gotten around to it before long.[2]

**When things I believe should happen, never happen.**

Doubts multiply when God says no to our prayers. When we pray for healing, but it doesn't come. When we pray for prodigals, but they don't return. When we ask, but we don't receive. When we seek, but we don't find. When we knock, but the sound of our bruised knuckles rapping on heaven's door gives only a hollow echo in reply.

**When things I believe should happen now, happen much later.**

Perhaps no answer is harder to carry away from the throne of grace than the word *wait*. When we're sure something is God's will and it's something He would delight in, we expect it to happen now—when we want it. But though God's will is for His kingdom to come to earth ushered in on our prayers, it will not come according to our timetable but according to His. And that, almost invariably, is much later than our faith is prepared for.

## Biblical Example: Abraham

This third category of events brings us to our passage for today, Hebrews 6:13–20. The writer has just exhorted us to be "imitators of those who through faith and patience inherit the promises" (v. 12). Now, in choosing Abraham, the writer is selecting a classic illustration of a man who waited and waited for a most unusual promise to occur.

> For when God made the promise to Abraham, since He could swear by no one greater, He swore by Himself, saying, "I will surely bless you, and I will surely multiply you." (vv. 13–14)

That promise was for a son to be born to Sarah, his wife. At the time the promise was given, she was sixty-five and Abraham was seventy-five. But by the time the promise was fulfilled, Abraham

2. Harold S. Kushner, *When Bad Things Happen to Good People* (New York, N.Y.: Avon Books, 1981), p. 6.

was one hundred and Sarah was ninety (17:17). Twenty-five years—a long time to wait for God to make good on His promise. But Abraham did wait, because God had sworn by His name to bring it to pass (compare 22:16–18).

> In hope against hope he believed, in order that he might become a father of many nations, according to that which had been spoken, "So shall your descendants be." And without becoming weak in faith he contemplated his own body, now as good as dead since he was about a hundred years old, and the deadness of Sarah's womb; yet, with respect to the promise of God, he did not waver in unbelief, but grew strong in faith, giving glory to God, and being fully assured that what He had promised, He was able also to perform. (Rom. 4:18–21)

In spite of twenty-four years of relative silence, God was faithful to keep His Word and to honor Abraham's faith.[3]

> And thus, having patiently waited, he obtained the promise. (Heb. 6:15)

## Spiritual Descendants: Heirs of the Promise

In verse 16 we come to a transitional principle that changes the subject from the character of Abraham to the custom of men.

> For men swear by one greater than themselves, and with them an oath given as confirmation is an end of every dispute.

In biblical times, men sealed their agreements with an oath, an oath based on a name greater than either of the two parties making the covenant. In the same way, God swore an oath that we might have encouragement in His promises.

> In the same way God, desiring even more to show to the heirs of the promise the unchangeableness of His purpose, interposed with an oath, in order that by two unchangeable things, in which it is impossible for God to lie, we may have strong encouragement. (vv. 17–18a)

---

3. Although Abraham wrestled with the mechanics of how God was going to fulfill His promise, he never doubted that the promise of a son would be fulfilled. His union with Hagar in Genesis 16 was a fumbled attempt to help facilitate faith—and that is always best accomplished by divine, not human, intervention.

Two theological facts surface in these verses. One: *God has a purpose for all of life.* Two: *God guarantees that purpose with an oath.*

Those are encouraging, aren't they? Regardless of how the times change, God's purpose for the believer is unchangeable. Regardless of how deceiving the circumstances are, God's Word is certain. Regardless of how shaky our situation, God is in control (see Ps. 46).

Three benefits that accrue to the believer who emulates Abraham's faith are mentioned in Hebrews 6:18–19.

> We who have fled for refuge in laying hold of the hope set before us. This hope we have as an anchor of the soul, a hope both sure and steadfast.

What obstacles to our faith do we encounter during the times when God is silent? Discouragement, despair, and doubt. And what do verses 18–19 offer to help us bear that silence? Strong encouragement, a refuge of hope, and an anchor of the soul.[4]

From a strictly human viewpoint, God's silence is often interpreted as desertion. Doubts collectively cup their hands and whisper in our ear: "God has forsaken you. You are all alone." But the last verses in Hebrews 6 shout over those gossipy innuendos.

> This hope we have as an anchor of the soul, a hope both sure and steadfast and one which enters within the veil,[5] where Jesus has entered as a forerunner for us, having become a high priest forever according to the order of Melchizedek. (vv. 19–20)

Jesus is our high priest—forever. We are never alone, no matter how deep or dark the valley (Ps. 23:4). He will never desert nor forsake us (Heb. 13:5b). And He will be with us always, even to the end of the age (Matt. 28:20)—and even to the end of our faith.

---

4. Though the metaphor of the anchor is widely used in ancient literature, its use here is the only time it appears in the entire New Testament. "Pythagoras said: 'Wealth is a weak anchor; fame is still weaker. What then are the anchors which are strong? Wisdom, great-heartedness, courage—these are the anchors which no storm can shake.' The writer to the Hebrews insists that the Christian possesses the greatest hope in the world." William Barclay, *The Letter to the Hebrews*, rev. ed., The Daily Study Bible Series (Philadelphia, Pa.: Westminster Press, 1976), p. 62.

5. The imagery takes us back to the Holy of Holies in the temple where only the high priest could enter on behalf of the people, and then only once a year. Jesus entered through the veil with the spotless sacrifice of His own life and placed it on the altar before God (Isa. 53:11). As a result, we have a hope that is both sure and steadfast that enables us to enter into the very throne room of God.

## When Dealing with Doubts, Remember

When on stormy seas, the tendency is to focus on the wind and the waves rather than on the Lord. That was Peter's problem, remember? The Lord called him out of the boat to walk where no man had ever walked before—on the water. And turbulent water at that. When Peter focused on Jesus, he was fine. But what happened when a wave slapped him in the face? He moved his eyes off the Savior and onto his circumstances (Matt. 14:27–31).

Amidst the storms of life—many of which are silent—God gives us an anchor for our soul. When doubt says, "You're a fool to believe," remember: God cannot lie. When doubt says, "You lose," remember: You will "overwhelmingly conquer" (Rom. 8:37). Even though the circumstances around you are puzzling and nothing seems to fit, the puzzle has a purpose. Finally, when doubt says, "You're alone," remember: Jesus doesn't leave you. Ever.

 *Living Insights* STUDY ONE

Hebrews 6:15 says of Abraham, "And thus, having patiently waited, he obtained the promise." It's easy to read right over two key words: *patiently waited.*

* Turn back to Genesis and learn more about Abraham's example of faith and patience. As you read chapters 17, 18, 21, and 22 of this first book of the Scriptures, write down a few of your observations regarding faith and patience as seen in Abraham's life.

| Abraham: Faith and Patience | |
|---|---|
| Verses | Observations |
| | |
| | |
| | |
| | |
| | |
| | |

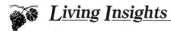 *Living Insights*

If we're honest with ourselves, we all must admit that we struggle with doubts from time to time. You've studied this subject today from a theoretical point of view. Now see if you can bring it to the level of your own heart.

- In your own life, what circumstances have caused you to doubt? Write down a few specifics.

  When things I believe should never happen, happen.

  _____

  _____

  _____

  _____

  _____

  When things I believe should happen, never happen.

  _____

  _____

  _____

  _____

  When things I believe should happen now, happen much later.

  _____

  _____

  _____

  _____

- In what way can the passages we've studied today help relieve those feelings of doubt about God's faithfulness?

Chapter 17

# MR. JONES, MEET MELCHIZEDEK

*Hebrews 7:1–19*

Just as beauty is in the eye of the beholder, so truth is often in the ear of the listener. The reason is, words mean different things to different people. Take the word *trunk*, for example. To a botanist, *trunk* means one thing. To an elephant trainer, it means something else. And to a professional mover, it means something entirely different.

Or how about the phrase *throwing a ball?* The same phrase can be used twice in the same newspaper but with altogether different meanings. In the sports page *throwing a ball* has a certain meaning for its readers, but on the society page the meaning is considerably different.

Similar variances in meanings arise when we come to the book of Hebrews, a book that many believe to be one of the most difficult in all the Bible.

## What Makes Hebrews So Difficult

The reason passages such as Hebrews 7:1–19 are so difficult to interpret is because the world in which its original readers lived was so different from our world today.

The original readers were people of Jewish heritage who had come to embrace Jesus as the Messiah. Today's readers of this letter, however, are mainly Gentiles. We have little acquaintance with Jewish traditions, the priesthood, or temple worship. We can hardly even pronounce names like Melchizedek, let alone understand their significance. In today's study we want to bridge that gap and introduce the modern-day Mr. Jones to the ancient-day Melchizedek. Before we do, however, let's review a couple of key facts about the book of Hebrews itself.

## Central Theme and Current Problem

The central theme of Hebrews is the superiority of Christ. He is the holy and exalted one, God's beloved Son who is superior to the prophets and the angels, our high priest forever representing us to the Father.

Because Jesus is supreme, He is worthy of our allegiance. Many of the first-century Hebrew converts, however, had become soft regarding Christ's superiority. They had become disillusioned and disoriented as a result of being persecuted, and many were seeking security by turning back to traditional ties—the Levitical priesthood, the Mosaic Law, the Old Covenant, ceremonial sacrifices, and ritual requirements.

The writer's warning to those retreating was, in a word, "Don't!" —because it was Jesus, not the priests, who was the solution to their problems. And with the coming of Jesus, a whole new era had dawned, eclipsing the Old Covenant traditions and leaving Judaism behind in the dark.

## Hope Is in Our High Priest, Jesus Christ

In showing the Hebrews that their hope is in a high priest who is totally unique, the writer uses their Jewish background to argue his case.

The point of reference is Melchizedek. The writer has already introduced us to this enigmatic person in 5:6 and 10, and 6:20. Obviously there is a close parallel between Jesus and Melchizedek, but it is difficult to discern the significance. Why? Because we live in a different world than did the first-century Hebrew convert. Let's seek a bridge between these worlds as we delve into chapter 7. There we will begin to unravel the knotted relationship that ties the two high priests together.

> For this Melchizedek, king of Salem, priest of the
> Most High God, who met Abraham as he was return-
> ing from the slaughter of the kings and blessed him,
> to whom also Abraham apportioned a tenth part of all
> the spoils,[1] was first of all, by the translation of his

1. "There is, beyond doubt, something momentous as well as mysterious about the occasion in the remote past when *this Melchizedek,* appearing unannounced on the scene, *met Abraham returning from the slaughter of the kings and blessed him.* The reference is to 'the battle of the four kings against five' described in Genesis 14:1ff. The four kings . . . carried off Lot, Abraham's nephew. . . . Abraham, on receiving news of this, . . . defeated the four kings and rescued Lot. . . . It was on his return from this excursion that the historic encounter with Melchizedek took place, when Melchizedek brought forth bread and wine for Abraham's refreshment and pronounced a blessing upon him, and Abraham presented tithes of all the spoils to Melchizedek. The obvious inference . . . is that in confrontation with Melchizedek, from whom he received the priestly benediction and to whom he paid homage, Abraham was face to face with one who was his superior." Philip Edgcumbe Hughes, *A Commentary on the Epistle to the Hebrews* (Grand Rapids, Mich.: William B. Eerdmans Publishing Co., 1977), p. 247.

name, king of righteousness, and then also king of Salem, which is king of peace.[2] Without father, without mother,[3] without genealogy,[4] having neither beginning of days nor end of life, but made like the Son of God, he abides a priest perpetually.

Now observe how great this man was to whom Abraham, the patriarch, gave a tenth of the choicest spoils. And those indeed of the sons of Levi who receive the priest's office have commandment in the Law to collect a tenth from the people, that is, from their brethren, although these are descended from Abraham. But the one whose genealogy is not traced from them collected a tenth from Abraham, and blessed the one who had the promises. But without any dispute the lesser is blessed by the greater. And in this case mortal men receive tithes, but in that case one receives them, of whom it is witnessed that he lives on. And, so to speak, through Abraham even Levi, who received tithes, paid tithes, for he was still in the loins of his father when Melchizedek met him. (vv. 1–10)

## Jesus and Melchizedek: Comparison

Melchizedek was the king of Salem, reigning over the region we now know as Jerusalem. Certainly we would think that a person with such impressive credentials would have an equally prestigious pedigree. But such was not the case. In the historical documentation in Genesis 14:18–20, nothing is noted regarding Melchizedek's parentage, ancestry, progeny, birth, or death. He seems to reign and carry on his priestly functions without beginning or end. As such, he is a fitting type of Christ, who ever lives and reigns and intercedes on our behalf.

2. From the Hebrew *shalom*, meaning "peace." Righteousness and peace were two qualities of the Messianic figure (see Isa. 9:6–7).

3. "The terms 'without father' and 'without mother' (*apatōr, amētōr*) are used in Greek for waifs of unknown parentage, for illegitimate children, for people who came from unimportant families. . . ." Leon Morris, "Hebrews," *The Expositor's Bible Commentary*, gen. ed. Frank E. Gaebelein (Grand Rapids, Mich.: Zondervan Publishing House, 1981), vol. 12, p. 63.

4. A priest's genealogy was of considerable importance. After the Exile, many of the priests whose genealogy could not be established were excluded from the priesthood as unclean (Neh. 7:64).

Although shrouded in mystery, Melchizedek was a great man for several reasons.[5] One, he collected a tithe from Abraham (Heb. 7:4–6a). Two, he blessed Abraham, the one who possessed the promises of God (v. 6b). And traditionally "it is always the superior who blesses the inferior."[6] Three, Melchizedek is declared the superior of the two (v. 7). Four, he "lives on," unlike the Levitical priests (vv. 8–10).

The recipients of this letter were trusting in the Levitical priesthood to give them the security and stability they were so desperately groping for. But the writer's point is that there was another priestly order superior to the Levitical line fathered by Aaron. It was the order of Melchizedek, a king-priest, who was a foreshadowing of a still greater future king and priest, the Lord Jesus Christ.

## Jesus and Moses: Contrast

In verse 11 the writer raises a crucial question, which he addresses in the verses that follow.

> Now if perfection was through the Levitical priesthood (for on the basis of it the people received the Law), what further need was there for another priest to arise according to the order of Melchizedek, and not be designated according to the order of Aaron? For when the priesthood is changed, of necessity there takes place a change of law also. For the one concerning whom these things are spoken belongs to another tribe, from which no one has officiated at the altar. For it is evident that our Lord was descended from Judah, a tribe with reference to which Moses spoke nothing concerning priests. (vv. 11–14)

The Levitical priesthood was inextricably bound to the Law. But before the Law was given, another type of priesthood existed. And it was *this* priesthood, the order of Melchizedek, that foreshadowed the high priesthood of Christ. Melchizedek represented something separate from the Law and something that the Levitical priesthood couldn't produce.

5. Some theologians view Melchizedek as a Christophany, a preincarnate appearance of Christ. But the passage in Hebrews 7:3 says he was "made *like* the Son of God" (emphasis added), not *was* the Son of God.

6. William Barclay, *The Letter to the Hebrews,* rev. ed., The Daily Study Bible Series (Philadelphia, Pa.: Westminster Press, 1976), p. 70.

In his commentary on the Greek text, Brooke Foss Westcott articulates the failure of the Levitical priesthood.

> If then there had been a bringing to perfection through the Levitical priesthood—if in other words there had been a bringing to perfection through the Law—there would have been no need of another priesthood. If on the other hand the whole Law failed to accomplish that to which it pointed, then so far also the priesthood failed. Such a failure, not a failure but the fulfillment of the divine purpose, was indicated by the promise of another priesthood in a new line.[7]

Besides failing to bring maturity into the life of the believer, the Law and the Levitical priesthood failed to give the believer access to God. But where the Old Covenant failed, the New Covenant succeeded. With Jesus there was the assurance both of growth to maturity (Heb. 12:1–2) and of unhindered access to God (Heb. 4:14–16).

Having descended from the tribe of Judah instead of Levi, Jesus stood outside the legal heritage for a priest of the Old Covenant. His priesthood, therefore, was of a completely different order. His priesthood was different in another way too. It was based on an indestructible life, patterned after Melchizedek.

> And this is clearer still, if another priest arises according to the likeness of Melchizedek, who has become such not on the basis of a law of physical requirement, but according to the power of an indestructible life. For it is witnessed of Him,
> "Thou art a priest forever
> According to the order of Melchizedek."
> (Heb. 7:15–17)

From beginning to end the Levitical priesthood was built around physical things. On the basis of physical blemishes a priest could be disqualified (Lev. 21:16–23). Even the ordination ceremony was dependent on physical observances like bathing in water, being clothed in prescribed garments, and being anointed with oil (Lev. 8). These physical observances were all draped around a life that could later become blemished and disqualified. But the new priesthood was built upon an indestructible life, without spot or blemish (Heb. 9:14)—upon One who ever lives to intercede for us (7:23–25).

---

7. *The Epistle to the Hebrews* (n.d.; reprint, Grand Rapids, Mich.: William B. Eerdmans Publishing Co., 1973), p. 180.

## Jesus and Me: Conclusion

We conclude our study today with a comparison the writer makes between the two covenants in verses 18–19.

> For, on the one hand, there is a setting aside of a former commandment because of its weakness and uselessness (for the Law made nothing perfect), and on the other hand there is a bringing in of a better hope, through which we draw near to God.

Jesus uprooted the Law which produced no fruit in the life of the believer, and He planted in its place the fragrant era of grace whose blossoms were redolent with hope. Whereas the Law was both weak and ineffective, grace was both effective and filled with assurance.

Remember, it is grace, not Law, which enables us to draw near to God. Security is not in a system of rigid rungs on some legalistic ladder to God. Security is in a Savior who has fulfilled the Law for us. Let's take a break now from the pedantic and take time to get personal. Do you want to be near to God? It doesn't take a moral make-over or a ceremonial cleansing of your life. You don't need a priestly pedigree. You don't need a heritage of people who have survived the rigors of religion and fought the good fight of perfect Sunday school attendance, putting up a pious front. You need a life that's indestructible. You need the only priest who lives permanently. You need Jesus Christ. For He can do for us what no earthly priest could.

First, Jesus not only knows where we're coming from but, more importantly, where we're going. And second, He's able to ensure that we get there, both in terms of our spiritual maturity and our eternal security. He not only cares where our head is, He cares where our heart is. For Him, indoctrination is not nearly as important as devotion. And third, Jesus not only tells us we are weak and empty in ourselves but, more importantly, how we can be strong and complete in Him. Apart from Him we can do nothing (John 15:4–5). But we can do all things through Him who strengthens us (Phil. 4:13, Gal. 2:16–20).

 *Living Insights* STUDY ONE

The key to understanding this passage is perspective. If we can put ourselves into the sandals of the first-century Hebrews, our appreciation of this passage will be heightened.

- Perhaps the best use of our time is to sort out the different descriptions of key characters in this passage. As you read through Hebrews 7:1–19, jot down significant observations regarding each of these people.

## Hebrews 7:1–19

### Melchizedek

Verse _____

Observation _____

_____

### Abraham

Verse _____

Observation _____

_____

### Levi

Verse _____

Observation _____

_____

### Aaron

Verse _____

Observation _____

_____

### Moses

Verse _____

Observation _____

_____

### Christ

Verse _____

Observation _____

_____

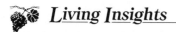 **Living Insights**

The topic of Melchizedek's priesthood presents many questions that baffle even the finest of theologians. It is not easy to interpret. How much understanding have you gained about this man? Take a shot at answering these questions.

- Who is Melchizedek?

  _____

  _____

- Does who he is make a difference? Why or why not?

  _____

  _____

- How does he compare to Christ?

  _____

  _____

- How does he compare to Abraham? To Aaron?

  _____

  _____

  _____

  _____

- What difference does the existence of Melchizedek make in your relationship with Christ?

  _____

  _____

- Name one item from this study that you can personally apply to your life.

  _____

  _____

  _____

**Chapter 18**

# A PERMANENT PONTIFEX

*Hebrews 7:18–28*

Setting up a comparison or contrast is a common literary device. Colleen McCullough utilizes this technique in her moving novel, *The Thorn Birds.*

In this epic drama that spans three generations, young Meggie Cleary grows up in the Australian outback under the protective wing of Father Ralph de Bricassart. As Meggie matures, her love for Father Ralph blossoms from platonic to romantic. But it is a love she will never be able to fulfill, for he is a priest, and his ambitions for the Vatican eclipse his emotions.

When Meggie finally comes to grips with the reality that Father Ralph will never leave the priesthood for her, she marries instead a rough-and-ready sheepshearer named Luke. But Luke, too, is driven by ambition—only his is to own one of the largest ranches in Australia. It is this ambition that drives him and Meggie apart.

Despite all their dissimilarities, Father Ralph and Luke had two things in common: a love for Meghann Cleary and an inner drive that caused them both, in their own separate ways, to sacrifice that love on the altar of ambition.

By placing these two characters side by side in the novel, the author enables us to see both their points of comparison and their points of contrast.

In a similar way, in the latter half of chapter 7, the author of Hebrews juxtaposes the Levitical priests with the priesthood of Jesus Christ.

## Declaration of Primary Objective

Verses 18–19 contrast the weakness of the Law with the strength of grace, the "better hope, through which we draw near to God."

It is this access to God—not the accumulation of religious merit badges—that transforms us from the inside out.[1] That is the writer's primary objective, to show us our access to God that we might *know* Him.

1. For an excellent book on this subject, read *Inside Out,* by Dr. Larry Crabb (Colorado Springs, Colo.: NavPress, 1988).

There's a world of difference between knowing *about* God and *knowing* God. You can know *about* God from having a degree in doctrine, but you can only *know* God from a devotion that draws you near to His heart.

Knowing God and having access to Him—these are the hall-marks of true religion.

But herein lies the problem. Between humanity and a holy God stretches an abyss that no amount of religious fervor or good deeds can span. What we need is a bridge.

The good news of Hebrews is that this "better hope, through which we draw near to God" is found in Jesus Christ (John 1:17). Through Him we have access to God (John 14:6). He is our *pontifex*, or our high priest, our bridge to God (1 Tim. 2:5, Heb. 8:6).[2] He is the one—the *only* one—who can open the way to God. And He does it permanently and perfectly. Once you know Him and approach God through Him, you never again need another human priest. He is the superior priest, a subject on which the writer spends the bulk of four chapters (7–10).

What makes Jesus superior is that He stands in contrast to all other priests. In fact, with the coming of Christ the priesthood became obsolete.

## Explanation of Jesus' Priesthood

A close reading of Hebrews 7:20–25 reveals that the author is utilizing the literary technique of comparison and contrast. The priestly office is the point of comparison between Jesus and the Levites. But the similarities end there.

> And it was not without an oath! Others became priests without any oath, but he became a priest with an oath when God said to him:
> "The Lord has sworn
> and will not change his mind:
> 'You are a priest forever.'"
> Because of this oath, Jesus has become the guarantee[3] of a better covenant.

2. The Latin term for priest is *pontifex* and means "bridge-builder," whose specific role is to build a bridge from God to man.

3. "Guarantee" is from the Greek word *egguos*. "An *egguos* is one who gives security. It is used, for instance, of a person who guarantees someone else's overdraft at a bank; he is surety that the money will be paid. It is used for someone who goes bail

Now there have been many of those priests, since death prevented them from continuing in office; but because Jesus lives forever, he has a permanent priesthood. Therefore he is able to save completely those who come to God through him, because he always lives to intercede for them.[4]

Between Jesus and all other priests, there are three contrasts that leap off the page.

| All Other Priests | Jesus |
|---|---|
| 1. There was no oath from God that established them as priests. All that entitled them to the office was their physical tie to the tribe of Levi (v. 20). | 1. Jesus' priesthood was established with an oath from God Himself (v. 21); see also Psalm 110, especially verse 4. |
| 2. Under the Old Covenant a guarantee was lacking. | 2. Under the New Covenant Jesus Himself is the guarantee (v. 22). |
| 3. The ministry of human priests was temporary; death prevented them from continuing (v. 23). | 3. The ministry of Jesus' priesthood is permanent;[5] he "abides forever" (v. 24) and "always lives to intercede for them" (v. 25). |

The reasons for Christ's superiority are found in verses 26–28.

Such a high priest meets our need—one who is holy, blameless, pure, set apart from sinners, exalted above the heavens. Unlike the other high priests, he does not need to offer sacrifices day after day, first for his own sins, and then for the sins of the people. He

---

for a prisoner; he guarantees that the prisoner will appear at the trial. The *egguos* is one who guarantees that some undertaking will be honoured." William Barclay, *The Letter to the Hebrews*, rev. ed., The Daily Study Bible Series (Philadelphia, Pa.: Westminster Press, 1976), p. 81.

4. The NIV Study Bible, New International Version (Grand Rapids, Mich.: Zondervan Bible Publishers, 1985).

5. "Permanently" is from the Greek word *aparabatos*. It is found nowhere else in the New Testament. In extra-biblical literature "*aparabatos* is a legal word. It means *inviolable*. A judge lays down that his decision must remain *aparabatos, unalterable*. It means *non-transferable*. . . . Galen, the medical writer, uses it to describe absolute scientific law which can never be violated, the principles on which the very universe is built and holds together." Barclay, *The Letter to the Hebrews*, p. 82.

sacrificed for their sins once for all when he offered himself. For the law appoints as high priests men who are weak; but the oath, which came after law, appointed the Son, who has been made perfect forever.[6]

Three reasons are cited. Jesus is superior because He is sinless (vv. 26–27a). He is superior because His sacrifice was offered once for all (v. 27b).[7] And He is superior because He is the perfect Son of God (v. 28).

## Application of Christ's Priesthood Today

Only through Christ can we reach God and know God. He is the way, the truth, and the life; no one comes to the Father but through Him (John 14:6). Neither does anyone know the Father without knowing Christ (v. 7).

If you're separated from God by what seems to be an unbridgeable chasm of sin, we have good news for you. You can reach God and know God through Jesus. He is the permanent pontifex. He is the perfect high priest. He is the bridge over the troubled water of sin that separates us from God.

If you need help understanding what Jesus did to erect that bridge between you and God, the following illustration should help. We hope it helps give you the clarity and understanding to reach out to God and take that first step of faith.

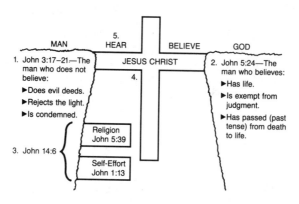

6. The NIV Study Bible, New International Version.

7. Jesus Himself was the sacrifice. He stretched Himself out over that altar and spilled His own blood to atone for sin (Heb. 9:24–28, 10:11–14). No other priests ever took the role of the sacrificial lamb—nor could they. He was the Lamb of God who took away the sins of the world (John 1:29, Isa. 53:10–12).

1. Man is separated from God and is under judgment because of sin (John 3:17–21, 36). (See also Romans 3:23, 6:23; Hebrews 9:27.)

2. The many statements made by Jesus about eternal life indicate there is a solution to this separation (John 5:24).

3. Man attempts to build his own bridges (1:13), but Jesus declares Himself to be the only Way (14:6). (See also Ephesians 2:8–9.)

4. Jesus is the Way because of who He is: God (John 1:14); the Lamb (1:36) . . . and because of what He did: He died (6:51; see also Romans 5:8); He rose from the dead (John 11:25).

5. Jesus calls on us to act on this message—to hear and believe (5:24). Synonyms: receive (1:12); be reborn (3:3); drink (4:13). (See also Revelation 3:20.)[8]

 *Living Insights*

There's a large amount of material in Hebrews regarding the priesthood. Are you comprehending this material? Taking another approach to this important concept may provide a clearer understanding.

- Read over Hebrews 7:18–28 in your own Bible. Next, locate some different translations or paraphrases of Scripture, and read through the same text in those versions. The differences may help you achieve a greater understanding of this passage. You may want to read back a few chapters too, using your favorite version, in order to shed some additional light on the subject of the priesthood.

---

8. Quote and illustration from *Living Proof*, by Jim Petersen (Colorado Springs, Colo.: NavPress, 1989), pp. 248–49. Used by permission.

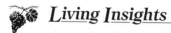 **_Living Insights_**

The primary objectives of true religion are _to know God and to have access to Him._ Read over that statement slowly and deliberately. Do you sense its heavy significance?

- Those two objectives appear simple on the surface, but are you sure you have them mastered? Give some serious thought, and perhaps some further Bible study, to the following questions.

  How do you get to know God?

  _____

  _____

  _____

  _____

  _____

  _____

  _____

  How can you gain access to Him?

  _____

  _____

  _____

  _____

  _____

  _____

## Chapter 19

# CHRIST'S COVENANT...
# NEW, NEVER OBSOLETE

### Hebrews 8:1–13

The high-tech age—it's wonderful, isn't it? One-inch TVs you can carry in the palm of your hand. Solar-powered calculators. Compact discs. Personal computers that can run a small city.

But there's one drawback. Six months after the hardware's developed for a new product, it becomes outdated, either superseded by a second generation of upgrades or innovated by the competition. It seems that just as you get your PC out of the box and booted up, it's rendered obsolete by some other computer that's faster, has more memory, more functions, better graphics, or is substantially cheaper.

Today we're going to unbox Christ's covenant from Hebrews 8. And the most exciting thing about this New Covenant is that, unlike today's technology, it will never become obsolete.

Ever.

## Christ's Priesthood: Better Than the Former

During the Old Covenant, priests from the tribe of Levi represented sinners before God, interceding on their behalf. Those who had sinned became cleansed through the innocent blood of animals that were sacrificed on the altar.

The problem with this method was that the effect was never final. No matter how qualified the priest, the blood he poured on the altar could only atone for the sins of the moment. The stirring message of Hebrews, however, is that Jesus is superior to those priests. Whereas the former priests offered blood, Jesus shed His own blood, atoning once for all for the sins of the world (10:11–12).

Christ's priesthood is better than the former because He is sinless, because His sacrifice was offered once, and because He is the perfect Son of God forever (7:26–28).

## Christ's Covenant: Better Than the Old

Our passage for today grows out of the fertile furrows of the last three verses of chapter 7. The first two verses of chapter 8 then spread like creeping tendrils to transition us from the subject of Christ's priesthood to Christ's covenant.

> Now the main point in what has been said is this: we have such a high priest, who has taken His seat at the right hand of the throne of the Majesty in the heavens, a minister in the sanctuary, and in the true tabernacle, which the Lord pitched, not man. (8:1–2)

Syntactically, there is a bold emphasis on the word *true* in the original Greek. The meaning of the term is "genuine" or "real." But the implication is not real as opposed to false, but real as opposed to a copy or representation. For example, a true dollar bill as opposed to a photocopied one, not a true dollar bill as opposed to a counterfeit.

The point is that the place where Christ ministers is the true tabernacle in its full reality. It is a tent pitched by God in heaven, not by man on earth (8:2, 9:24).

This means there has to be a new arrangement between God and humankind. Before, earthly priests represented sinful man in the Holy of Holies in an earthly tent. Now, a heavenly priest represents us in heaven before the very throne of God. If we have a new priest who is superior to the old, it stands to reason that we have a new covenant or arrangement that is also superior to the old.

Verses 3–12 of chapter 8 describe the new arrangement. And in verses 3–9 we are given two reasons why this arrangement is better.

First: *This New Covenant is a reality, not a representation.*

> For every high priest is appointed to offer both gifts and sacrifices; hence it is necessary that this high priest also have something to offer. Now if He were on earth, He would not be a priest at all, since there are those who offer the gifts according to the Law; who serve a copy and shadow of the heavenly things, just as Moses was warned by God when he was about to erect the tabernacle; for, "See," He says, "that you make all things according to the pattern which was shown you on the mountain." (vv. 3–5)

Just as a shadow has to be cast by some substance, so the rituals of the Old Covenant are representative of a greater reality.

> The Greeks were fascinated by this conception of a real world of which this world is only a flickering, imperfect copy. In this world we walk in shadows; somewhere there is reality. The great problem in life

is how to pass from this world of shadows to the other world of realities. That is the idea of which the writer to the Hebrews makes use.

The earthly Temple is a pale copy of the real Temple of God; earthly worship is a remote reflection of real worship; the earthly priesthood is an inadequate shadow of the real priesthood. All these things point beyond themselves to the reality of which they are the shadows. The writer to the Hebrews even finds that idea in the Old Testament itself. When Moses had received from God instructions about the construction of the tabernacle and all its furnishings, God said to him: "And see that you make them after the pattern for them, which is being shown you on the mountain" (Exodus 25:40). God had shown Moses the real pattern of which all earthly worship is the ghost-like copy. So then the writer to the Hebrews says that the earthly priests have a service which is but a *shadowy outline* of the heavenly order. For *shadowy outline* he combines two Greek words, *hupodeigma*, which means *a specimen*, or, still better, a sketch-plan, and *skia*, which means *a shadow*, a reflection, a phantom, a silhouette.[1]

Second: *This New Covenant is faultless, not faulty.*

But now He has obtained a more excellent ministry, but as much as He is also the mediator of a better covenant, which has been enacted on better promises. For if that first covenant had been faultless, there would have been no occasion sought for a second. For finding fault with them, He says,

> "Behold, days are coming, says the Lord,
> When I will effect a new covenant
> With the house of Israel and with the
>     house of Judah;
> Not like the covenant which I made with
>     their fathers
> On the day when I took them by the
>     hand
> To lead them out of the land of Egypt;
> For they did not continue in My covenant,

1. William Barclay, *The Letter to the Hebrews*, rev. ed., The Daily Study Bible Series (Philadelphia, Pa.: Westminster Press, 1976), p. 88.

And I did not care for them, says the
Lord. (Heb. 8:6–9)

These verses don't imply that the Old Covenant was sinful, only
that it was insufficient. The Law reflected the righteousness of God,
but it couldn't produce righteousness in the believer's life. But where
the Old Covenant wilted when it came to imparting life, the New
Covenant blossomed with the vitalizing fragrance of forgiveness.

The remainder of Hebrews 8 enumerates why this New Covenant
is better than the old one.

First: *It offers internal motivation and power instead of external lists.*

> "For this is the covenant that I will make
>     with the house of Israel
> After those days, says the Lord:
> I will put My laws into their minds,
> And I will write them upon their hearts."
> (v. 10a)

If you've ever felt inadequate, ever felt you couldn't measure up
to the righteous standards of God, this verse should be a real encouragement (see also 2 Cor. 3:1–6).

Second: *It is based on a close relationship instead of one that is fearful
and distant.*

> "And I will be their God,
> And they shall be My people."
> (Heb. 8:10b)

If you've ever felt afraid of God and kept your distance from
Him, this verse should be a great comfort. He has taken us under
the shelter of His soft, gentle wing, to nurture and protect us.

Third: *It provides confidence and assurance instead of insecurity and
uncertainty.*

> "And they shall not teach everyone his
>     fellow citizen,
> And everyone his brother, saying, 'Know
>     the Lord,'
> For all shall know Me,
> From the least to the greatest of them."
> (v. 11)

If you've doubted with trembling knees, never quite knowing
where you stand with God, verse 11 plants your feet solidly in His
kingdom's soil—not as a transient or an illegal alien, but as a *citizen!*

132

Fourth: *It emphasizes forgiveness and mercy instead of failure and wrong.*

> "For I will be merciful to their iniquities,
> And I will remember their sins no more."
> (v. 12)

If you're in a prison of guilt and have realized the truth of Romans 3:19–23—that you've sinned and fallen woefully short of God's glory—then Hebrews 8:12 is the key that offers welcome release (compare Eph. 2:1–9).

The writer concludes Hebrews 8 with the word we used to introduce our study—*obsolete.*

> When He said, "A new covenant," He has made the first obsolete. But whatever is becoming obsolete and growing old is ready to disappear. (v. 13)

As the writer pens his letter, the shadows created by the Old Covenant have already lengthened. An obsolete era in biblical history is sinking below the horizon.

### Christ's Life: Better Than the Flesh

The bad news is that we've all made a mess of our lives and fallen short of the glory of God. The good news is that Jesus can take that spilled milk and turn it into ice cream. And that's why Christ's life is better than the life of the flesh. The flesh is incapable of cleansing itself. The Law functions as a mirror to reveal our sins, but it can only condemn; it can't cleanse. Only Jesus can take the dark stains that have set indelibly in our flesh and wash them white as snow (1 John 1:9).

That's grace. That's amazing grace. And that's a sweet sound to ears that have heard only hard accusations from the stone tablets of the Law.

 *Living Insights*

When Christ replaced the high priests, there came a need for a new covenant or, as we called it in our study, the new arrangement. Let's place these two covenants side by side and, as you read through Hebrews 8, 9, and 10, copy down descriptions of them both on the following page. The contrast between the two should become self-evident.

## Hebrews 8–10

| Old Covenant | New Covenant |
|---|---|
| _____ | _____ |
| _____ | _____ |
| _____ | _____ |
| _____ | _____ |
| _____ | _____ |
| _____ | _____ |
| _____ | _____ |

### *Living Insights* STUDY TWO

The contrast between the Old and New Covenants provides us with an excellent occasion to look at the contrasts between our old life and our new life in Christ. Write down some traits from your old life and the contrasts seen in your new life of grace. Then close by praying through 2 Corinthians 5:7–17, thanking God for making all things new.

### The Contrasts in My Life

| The Old Life | The New Life |
|---|---|
| _____ | _____ |
| _____ | _____ |
| _____ | _____ |
| _____ | _____ |
| _____ | _____ |
| _____ | _____ |
| _____ | _____ |

## Chapter 20

# MAY I SPEAK TO YOUR CONSCIENCE, PLEASE?

### Hebrews 9:1–14

In his excellent commentary on Hebrews, William Barclay prefaces his discussion of chapter 9 with these words:

> The writer to the Hebrews has just been thinking of Jesus as the one who leads us into reality. He has been using the idea that in this world we have only pale copies of what is truly real. The worship that men can offer is only a ghost-like shadow of the real worship which Jesus, the real High Priest, alone can offer. But even as he thinks of that his mind goes back to the Tabernacle (the Tabernacle, remember, not the Temple). Lovingly he remembers its beauty; lovingly he lingers on its priceless possessions. And the thought in his mind is this—if earthly worship was as beautiful as this, what must the true worship be like? If all the loveliness of the Tabernacle was only a shadow of reality, how surpassingly lovely the reality must be. He does not tell of the Tabernacle in detail; he only alludes to certain of its treasures. This was all he needed to do because his readers knew its glories and had them printed on their memories. But we do not know them; therefore, let us see what the beauty of the earthly Tabernacle was like, always remembering that it was only a pale copy of reality.[1]

Today we want to take a closer look at the tabernacle and a closer look at our own conscience as well.

## Internal-External Distinction: Clarification

Before we take apart the nuts and bolts of the tabernacle, let's take a closer look at the conscience. The Bible makes a clear distinction between the material part of our lives and the immaterial part (Eccles. 12:7). Externally, we have a body that can be touched and

---

1. William Barclay, *The Letter to the Hebrews*, rev. ed., The Daily Study Bible Series (Philadelphia, Pa.: Westminster Press, 1976), pp. 94–95.

handled. Internally, we have a conscience that, although it can't be touched, touches us. It can reward or reproach us, congratulate or condemn us, applaud or accuse us. Our conscience can either rub up softly against us or prick us like a porcupine, depending on how we have first treated it.

Both testaments show a distinction between the internal and external realities.

> "God sees not as man sees, for man looks at the outward
> appearance, but the Lord looks at the heart."
> (1 Sam. 16:7)

> Though our outer man is decaying, yet our inner man
> is being renewed day by day. (2 Cor. 4:16)[2]

Within our bodies is a reticulated weave of feelings and impulses. Somehow the soul and the will and the spirit are all interwoven with this strong thread we call the conscience. Though its voice is still and small within us, it reverberates throughout our entire soul. And it can be as painful as it is pervasive.

In Hebrews 9:14 the pain that's talked about is a remorse for "dead works." The problem with the Hebrews was that they tried to quiet their conscience with religious activity. But their efforts were futile, because you can't solve internal unrest with external involvement. To illustrate his point, the writer sketches in our minds not only the layout of the tabernacle but also its lesson.

## External Regulations: The Tabernacle

The first ten verses of Hebrews 9 deal with the tabernacle and fall into two distinct divisions: first, the layout of the tabernacle and its worship (vv. 1–5); then, its regulations (vv. 6–10).

### The Arrangement of the Furniture

The tabernacle was a tent the Israelites carried with them during their wilderness wanderings so that whenever and wherever they stopped, they would be able to erect a place of worship.[3] It was a temporary, portable structure, and within it, a variety of furnishings were arranged in such a way as to stimulate their worship of God.

> Now even the first covenant had regulations of
> divine worship and the earthly sanctuary. For there

---

2. See also Matthew 10:28 and Luke 16:15.

3. The main description of the tabernacle is found in Exodus 25–31 and 35–40.

was a tabernacle prepared, the outer one, in which were the lampstand and the table and the sacred bread; this is called the holy place. And behind the second veil, there was a tabernacle which is called the Holy of Holies, having a golden altar of incense and the ark of the covenant covered on all sides with gold, in which was a golden jar holding the manna, and Aaron's rod which budded, and the tables of the covenant. And above it were the cherubim of glory overshadowing the mercy seat; but of these things we cannot now speak in detail. (vv. 1–5)

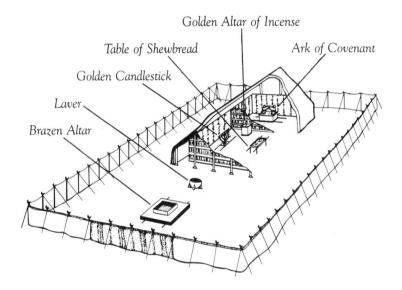

Golden Altar of Incense

Table of Shewbread

Golden Candlestick

Ark of Covenant

Laver

Brazen Altar

### Activities of the Priest

In verses 6–10 the attention shifts from the placement of furniture to the practice of the priest.

Now when these things have been thus prepared, the priests are continually entering the outer tabernacle, performing the divine worship, but into the second only the high priest enters, once a year, not without taking blood, which he offers for himself and for the sins of the people committed in ignorance. The Holy Spirit is signifying this, that the way into the holy place has not yet been disclosed, while the outer tabernacle is still standing, which is a symbol for the present

137

time. Accordingly both gifts and sacrifices are offered which cannot make the worshiper perfect in con-science, since they relate only to food and drink and various washings, regulations for the body imposed until a time of reformation.

There was nothing wrong with ritual. But ritual—however resplendent—changed nothing *within* a person. It could not perfect the conscience of the worshiper (v. 9), as it related only to the external part of man ("for the body," v. 10).

Also, the ritual was a symbol that represented something greater than itself. It was something like a religious drama enacted before an audience of the entire nation of Israel. But the drama itself was not reality; it merely pointed to reality. It was "only a shadow of the good things to come and not the very form of things" (10:1).

The Hebrews in the first century were returning to this ritualistic activity between priests and people, hoping to find in it that inner relief of a clear conscience. But activity—no matter how religious—can't appease the dictates of a troubled conscience.

Activity is often only a hasty anesthetic to take the sharp edge off the pain of a prickly conscience. But although it can deaden the pain, it can't heal the hurt deep inside. And just as some people get addicted to painkillers, so others get addicted to activity.

Another thing we get addicted to is tangibles—things we can see and feel. Somehow, we tend to feel better surrounded by religious icons. For an example, look back to Numbers 21:4–9 and study the healing that God ordained through a bronze serpent. Then turn to 2 Kings 18:1–4. Almost eight hundred years later, the people were still dragging around and burning incense to that "piece of bronze."

In a similar way, we attach almost mystical and supernatural significance to our own religious symbols, whether a massive window of stained glass, a gilded cross, or a stone statue. There's nothing wrong with symbols—as long as the fixation is on the things they represent and not the things themselves.

### Internal Restoration: The Christ

Many of the Hebrews thought that if they could just get back to a secure routine of religious ritual, somehow their conscience could be cleansed. But the writer dispels that notion by saying, essentially, that you can't use an *external* solution for an *internal* problem. That problem, he tells us in 9:11–14, can only be solved by Jesus Christ.

But when Christ appeared as a high priest of the good things to come, He entered through the greater and more perfect tabernacle, not made with hands, that is to say, not of this creation; and not through the blood of goats and calves, but through His own blood, He entered the holy place once for all, having obtained eternal redemption. For if the blood of goats and bulls and the ashes of a heifer sprinkling those who have been defiled, sanctify for the cleansing of the flesh, how much more will the blood of Christ, who through the eternal Spirit offered Himself without blemish to God, cleanse your conscience from dead works to serve the living God?

When Jesus died, arose, and ascended, He replaced the temporary symbol with a permanent reality.

These verses delineate several things regarding the priestly ministry of Christ. First, the tabernacle He entered as our high priest was *not* made with human hands; it wasn't a tangible thing. Second, the blood He brought to the altar was *not* that of animals; it was His own. Third, His sacrifice provided a permanent solution for sin; it was an "eternal redemption," . . . "once for all" (v. 12).

Because the redemption was eternal and was offered for all, it is ours to claim. And if the blood of goats and bulls cleansed the flesh in those ancient days, how much more does the blood of Christ cleanse us!

And what does it cleanse? Our conscience.

## Appropriating Internal Changes

The question that relates to us in the harried pace of the twentieth century is, How? How do we get off the freeway of rush-hour religious traffic? Where do we pull off the road to get directions? Where do we exit?

Well, here are a couple of guidelines to help steer you in the right direction. First: *Stop emphasizing the externals.* Get rid of a ritualistic religious experience. Quit going through empty motions. Give up religion by rote. And get rid of any symbols that have become objects of worship.

Second: *Start focusing on the internals.* Look beyond the shadow of the symbols to the substance they represent. Focus on the things God does—on the inside (1 Sam. 16:7). Look to Christ, fix your eyes on Him (Heb. 12:2). When you do, the things of this world, as the hymn says, will indeed "grow strangely dim in the light of His glory and grace." Even your feverish activity for Him will pale in the light of what He has done. Because what He has done for you is infinitely more than you could ever do for Him.

 **_Living Insights_** STUDY ONE

Our study pointed out the distinction between externals and internals. We looked briefly at 1 Samuel 16:7, which says, "'God sees not as man sees, for man looks at the outward appearance, but the Lord looks at the heart.'"

- Immediately following 1 Samuel 16 is the story of David and Goliath, found in chapter 17. As you read this well-known story, look for externals and internals and record them below.

### 1 Samuel 17: David and Goliath

| Externals | Internals |
| --- | --- |
| | |
| | |
| | |
| | |
| | |
| | |
| | |
| | |
| | |
| | |
| | |
| | |
| | |
| | |
| | |
| | |

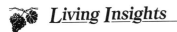 *Living Insights*

After a message of this nature, you may find yourself asking the question, How can I get off this religious merry-go-round and begin appropriating the true significance of Christ's death? Maybe answering the following related questions and statements will help.

- Write down the religious externals that you tend to emphasize in your life.

_____

_____

_____

_____

- Why do you have the tendency to stress each of these externals?

_____

_____

_____

_____

- Write down the internals that should command more of your focus.

_____

_____

_____

_____

- How can you appropriate these internals into your lifestyle?

_____

_____

_____

_____

## Chapter 21

# SIGNED, SEALED, DELIVERED . . . IN BLOOD

*Hebrews 9:15–28*

Henry David Thoreau's timeless essay, "Life without Principle," gives two different ways of viewing a forest.

> If a man walk in the woods for love of them half of each day, he is in danger of being regarded as a loafer; but if he spends his whole day as a speculator, shearing off those woods and making earth bald before her time, he is esteemed an industrious and enterprising citizen. As if a town had no interest in its forests but to cut them down![1]

Just as a speculator looks at a forest and sees only the economic value of the trees, so a Bible expositor often looks at a majestic forest of revelation like Hebrews and sees only the exegetical value of individual phrases and words.

Sadly, the awe of standing at the base of a giant redwood is often obscured on Sunday mornings by a too-close look at the bark. A walk in the forest *should* fill our souls with wonder. And a walk through the stately truths of Scripture should do the same.

So with that perspective in mind, let's take a stroll through the second half of Hebrews 9, just for the love of it . . . and for the love of the Savior to whom these verses perennially lift their boughs in praise!

## Some Reminders about Hebrews

Humanity has been likened to a man who stumbled into a well. As he treaded water, he called out for help. Responding to the call, a passerby stopped, leaned over, and asked the man what he wanted. The man said he wanted out. The passerby thought a moment, wrote on a piece of paper, then dropped it down to the struggling man. It read: "Ten Rules on How to Keep Out of Wells."

---

1. Henry David Thoreau, "Life without Principle," *Thoreau: Walden and Other Writings,* ed. Joseph Wood Krutch (New York, N.Y.: Bantam Books, 1971), p. 356.

That's the type of help the Law gives us. It is prescriptive—not curative. It can advise us how to keep out of wells, but it's powerless to let down a rope to save us from drowning.

The message of Hebrews is that life is infinitely more than treading water in the bottom of a well. And to those struggling to get out, the writer introduces the only individual who is able to lean over and lower a rope—Jesus Christ.

Because of this, Jesus is superior to any individual, to the Law, and to the Old Testament priesthood. Under the old arrangement, sins were only temporarily forgiven. Under the new arrangement, deliverance from sin's penalty becomes permanent. That's what makes Jesus superior.

Consequently, our hope is not in the things we need to do, but in what Christ already did. Like a giant red arrow, the letter to the Hebrews points us to Christ, and in doing so, diverts attention from ourselves.

It is this new arrangement, this new covenant, that should occupy us—not the old ways, the old regulations, the old rules. Hebrews 9:13–15a makes clear the distinction.

> For if the blood of goats and bulls and the ashes of a heifer sprinkling those who have been defiled, sanctify for the cleansing of the flesh, how much more will the blood of Christ, who through the eternal Spirit offered Himself without blemish to God, cleanse your conscience from dead works to serve the living God? And for this reason He is the mediator of a new covenant.

Under the old arrangement, the blood of animals was required. Under the new arrangement, the blood of animals was replaced by the blood of God's Lamb—Jesus Christ.

## The Essential Issue: Blood

In verses 15–28, the idea of blood is tied to three specifics: covenant (vv. 15–21), forgiveness (v. 22), and salvation (vv. 23–28).

### Blood, as it relates to covenant.

The term *covenant* is used six times in verses 15–21, but it is used in two different ways. In verses 16–17, the idea is that of a will, as in "last will and testament." In the other verses, it could be translated "arrangement."[2]

2. "Up to verse 16 the writer to the Hebrews has been using *diathēkē* in the normal Christian sense of *covenant*; then, suddenly and without warning or explanation, he

And for this reason He is the mediator of a new [arrangement], in order that since a death has taken place for the redemption of the transgressions that were committed under the first [arrangement], those who have been called may receive the promise of the eternal inheritance. For where a [will] is, there must of necessity be the death of the one who made it. For a [will] is valid only when men are dead, for it is never in force while the one who made it lives. Therefore even the first [arrangement] was not inaugurated without blood. For when every commandment had been spoken by Moses to all the people according to the Law, he took the blood of the calves and the goats, with water and scarlet wool and hyssop, and sprinkled both the book itself and all the people, saying, "This is the blood of the [arrangement] which God commanded you." And in the same way he sprinkled both the tabernacle and all the vessels of the ministry with the blood.

The rationale for the old arrangement is found in Leviticus 17:11.

"For the life of the flesh is in the blood, and I have given it to you on the altar to make atonement for your souls; for it is the blood by reason of the life that makes atonement."

What was true in the old arrangement is equally true of the new—there must be a death for the will to be activated. In order to settle sin's sprawling estate, Jesus Christ had to die. We are the beneficiaries of that death, and what we inherit is forgiveness.

### Blood, as it relates to forgiveness.

Germinating within Hebrews 9:22 is a seed of truth that enshells in kernel form all the theology of both the New and Old Testaments.

And according to the Law, one may almost say, all things are cleansed with blood, and without shedding of blood there is no forgiveness.

---

switches to the sense of *will*. . . . This founding of an argument on a play between two meanings of a word was a favourite method of the Alexandrian scholars in the time when this letter was written. In fact this very argument would have been considered in the days when the letter to the Hebrews was written an exceedingly clever piece of exposition." William Barclay, *The Letter to the Hebrews*, rev. ed., The Daily Study Bible Series (Philadelphia, Pa.: Westminster Press, 1976), p. 107.

The verse is an echo not only of Leviticus 17:11, but also of Christ's own words in Matthew 26:28.

> For this is My blood of the covenant, which is poured
> out for many for forgiveness of sins.

Two critical points of theology pivot on Hebrews 9:22. First: *Sin is a terrible offense.* It's not simply an indiscretion. It can't be watered down with smooth, fluid words like *weakness . . . shortcoming . . . mistake.* Sin is a heinous act of transgression against a holy God. There is an insidious, serpent-like hiss to the word, and through the white hollow of its fangs flows deadly poison.

The second point of theology found in verse 22 is that *forgiveness is a costly thing.* A holy God can't wink at sin. He can't turn His head the other way. He can't dismiss it with the backhanded wave of a grandfatherly hand and say, "Boys will be boys." No. If sin is a terrible offense, it follows necessarily that forgiveness has to be costly in order to pay for the damages. The proof of the awfulness of sin is that God required the shedding of blood for its atonement.

### Blood, as it relates to salvation.

All the blood sacrifices of the Mosaic system were like a hastily drawn pencil sketch when compared to the Sistine Chapel ceilings of heaven where the blood of Christ's sacrifice was poured upon the altar of God.

The value of the earthly sacrifices lay in the fact that they portrayed heavenly truth. As good and essential as these sacrifices were, there awaited one in heaven that was far better.[3]

> Therefore it was necessary for the copies of the
> things in the heavens to be cleansed with these, but
> the heavenly things themselves with better sacrifices
> than these. For Christ did not enter a holy place made
> with hands, a mere copy of the true one, but into

---

3. "Once a year the tabernacle had to be cleansed. It was only a copy of the true heavenly tabernacle (9:23). Nonetheless once a year on the day of atonement Israel's high priest had to go through a most elaborate ceremony so that, as God put it, 'In this way he will make atonement for the Most Holy Place because of the uncleanness and rebellion of the Israelites, whatever their sins have been. He is to do the same for the Tent of Meeting, which is among them in the midst of their uncleanness' (Lv. 16:16). By this means, then, God made his point to ancient Israel. They were alerted to the fact that they were sinful and that only by the shedding of blood could the tabernacle be cleansed and God be enabled to remain dwelling among them." David Gooding, *An Unshakeable Kingdom* (Grand Rapids, Mich.: William B. Eerdmans Publishing Co., 1989), p. 191.

> heaven itself, now to appear in the presence of God
> for us; nor was it that He should offer Himself often,
> as the high priest enters the holy place year by year
> with blood not his own. Otherwise, He would have
> needed to suffer often since the foundation of the
> world; but now once at the consummation of the ages
> He has been manifested to put away sin by the sacrifice
> of Himself. (vv. 23–26)

Two strong contrasts are presented in verses 24–26. First, Christ didn't enter a holy place made with hands, but rather heaven itself. Second, Christ didn't offer up sacrifices often, as did the other high priests, but only once. And that one sacrifice was effective for all time.

Chapter 9 concludes with a word of warning to those not ready (v. 27) and a word of encouragement to those eagerly awaiting His return (v. 28).

> And inasmuch as it is appointed for men to die once
> and after this comes judgment, so Christ also, having
> been offered once to bear the sins of many, shall appear
> a second time for salvation without reference to sin,
> to those who eagerly await Him.

The Epicurean motto was "Eat, drink, and be merry, for tomorrow we die." Translated in modern-day vernacular: You only go around once in life, so grab all the gusto while you can. The philosophy doesn't sound so antiquarian when you dress up the ad copy, does it?

The world view of the writer to the Hebrews is substantially different from the vantage point of a high rise on Madison Avenue. The words "and after this comes judgment" don't sell well with the consuming public.

The Bible looks at life—and the afterlife—from a different angle. As Solomon discovered, there is more to life than eating, drinking, and being merry (see Eccles. 2). And there is more to death than the grave. Beyond the grave there is God. Waiting for us. Eagerly. Like a father awaiting the reunion of all his children. The real question is, Are we eagerly awaiting Him? Do we yearn to see His eyes? Do we ache for His embrace? Do we long to hear the words, "Well done, good and faithful servant?"

Don't let anything stand in the way of that homecoming experience, will you? The glorious good news shouted from the rooftops of Hebrews 9 is that *judgment is escapable because today's sin is forgivable.* That's the kind of news that makes you want to come home, wherever you've been—and for however long you've been gone.

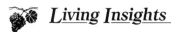 

The New Covenant is an exciting biblical promise! Hebrews 9 is filled with important words that need our understanding in order for us to fully grasp the genius of this new arrangement.

- Using the key words from Hebrews 9:15–28 as a springboard, briefly describe how these elements relate to your life.

### Hebrews 9:15–28—Significance to My Life

*Mediator* (v. 15)

_____

_____

_____

*Covenant* (v. 15)

_____

_____

_____

*Transgressions* (v. 15)

_____

_____

_____

*Inheritance* (v. 15)

_____

_____

_____

*Forgiveness* (v. 22)

_____

_____

_____

*Sacrifices* (v. 23)

_____

_____

_____

*Judgment* (v. 27)

_____

_____

_____

*Salvation* (v. 28)

_____

_____

_____

 *Living Insights*            STUDY TWO

The conclusion of this message capsulizes the Christian's hope. To know that sin is forgivable and judgment is escapable causes us to sigh in welcome relief.

- Let's spend our time today talking with God. Your agenda before the Father will be unique. You may spend the time in praise and thanks for the promise of forgiveness. Or, you may pray in confession and repentance. Whatever the case, use this as an occasion to come boldly before God's gracious throne to lay your burdens down.

## Chapter 22

# ONE FOR ALL, ONCE FOR ALL, FREE FOR ALL

*Hebrews 10:1–18*

Have you ever noticed how boring and repetitious a strict diet is? Half a grapefruit. Dry toast. A cup of black coffee. Doesn't sound like much of a breakfast, does it? Yet morning after lackluster morning that's what you have to look forward to if you want to make any progress fighting the battle of the bulge.

In a similar way, the routine ritual of the Law was often monotonous and dull. Everything was prescribed—how the priest was to be dressed, how the animals were to be sacrificed, what kind of offering was to be used for specific rituals.

There was no room for freedom or creativity. The priests couldn't slip into something a little more stylish, the type of sacrifice couldn't be varied, and the feast days couldn't be changed around to fit your schedule. No, the Law was quite precise about its prescriptions.

Yet, at the same time, it was ephemeral in nature. The Law was merely a shadow cast by the good things on the horizon of grace. Like a cookbook, it represented something far greater than itself. Cookbooks don't satisfy the taste, fill the stomach, or nourish the body. Instead, they point to something beyond themselves—food.

What the meal is to the cookbook, Jesus Christ is to the Law. That's the message of our passage today, Hebrews 10:1–18.

## Limitations of the Law

Look closely at verses 1–4, and you'll find some very obvious limitations to the Law.

> For the Law, since it has only a shadow[1] of the
> good things to come and not the very form[2] of things,

---

1. "The word he uses is *skia*, the Greek for a *shadow*, and it means a nebulous reflection, a mere silhouette, a form without reality." William Barclay, *The Letter to the Hebrews*, rev. ed., The Daily Study Bible Series (Philadelphia, Pa.: Westminster Press, 1976), p. 112.

2. "The word he uses is *eikōn*, which means a *complete representation*, *a detailed reproduction*. It actually does mean a *portrait*, and would mean a *photograph*, if there

can never by the same sacrifices year by year, which they offer continually, make perfect those who draw near. Otherwise, would they not have ceased to be offered, because the worshipers, having once been cleansed, would no longer have had consciousness of sins?[3] But in those sacrifices there is a reminder of sins year by year. For it is impossible for the blood of bulls and goats to take away sins.

The first limitation is: *The Law can never make anyone perfect* (v. 1). The type of cleansing offered was ceremonial; it assured a conformity of a person's exterior life but provided no power to change things inside.

The second limitation is: *It cannot permanently take away sins.* Underscore the word *impossible* in verse 4. The Law couldn't offer continual cleansing; its benefits were only temporary.

If the sacrifices did anything permanently, it was to make an indelible impression of how temporary its benefits were (v. 3). And in reminding people of that, it also reminded them of their guilt. Just as a speed limit sign sensitizes us to our guilt when we drive too fast, so the Law reminds us of our transgressions (Rom. 3:20–23). In the repetition of those sacrifices there was a reminder that all humanity has been weighed in the balance and found wanting, that we all fall short of the glory of God—daily, yearly, and eternally.

## Contrasts of the Christ

Quoting from Psalm 40:6–8, the writer places sacrifices in their proper context. In doing so, the contrast between the sacrifices and Christ stands out in bold relief.

> Therefore, when He comes into the world, He says,
> "Sacrifice and offering Thou hast not desired,
> But a body Thou hast prepared for Me;

---

had been such a thing in those days. In effect he is saying: 'Without Christ you cannot get beyond the shadows of God.'" Barclay, *The Letter to the Hebrews*, pp. 112–13.

3. "At no point did they feel that the price of sin had finally been paid completely. If they had, they would not have offered another sacrifice ever. After all, you don't keep on paying monthly instalments when the mortgage on your house has been completely paid off." David Gooding, *An Unshakeable Kingdom* (Grand Rapids, Mich.: William B. Eerdmans Publishing Co., 1989), p. 199.

> In whole burnt offerings and sacrifices
> for sin Thou hast taken no pleasure.
> "Then I said, 'Behold, I have come
> (In the roll of the book it is written of
> Me)
> To do Thy will, O God.'"
>
> After saying above, "Sacrifices and offerings and whole
> burnt offerings and sacrifices for sin Thou hast not
> desired, nor hast Thou taken pleasure in them" (which
> are offered according to the Law), then He said, "Be-
> hold, I have come to do Thy will." He takes away the
> first in order to establish the second. By this will we
> have been sanctified through the offering of the body
> of Jesus Christ once for all. (Heb. 10:5–10)

First: *In contrast to the offering of animals for sacrifice, Jesus offered
His own body.* The burnt carcass of a brute creature brought no
lasting satisfaction before an eternal altar that cried out for justice.
The reason? No will was involved. In fact, it was *against* the will of
the animal. At best, the animal would stand in ignorance and submit
to the knife. Here's where the contrast with Christ stands out so
magnificently. With Jesus, a *will* was involved—a will that submitted
obediently to God (compare v. 9a with Matt. 26:42).

It is because of this will, submitted to the will of the Father,
that we are *sanctified* (v. 10). The word means "set apart for its
intended purpose." That's something the Law couldn't do. It could
set us aside to be shunned or to be stoned, but it couldn't set us
apart to achieve the fullest purpose for which we had been created.
And we fulfill that purpose when we follow Christ's footsteps to the
altar of sacrifice (Rom. 12:1–2).

The second contrast is found in verses 11–14: *He made one offering
rather than many.*

> And every priest stands daily ministering and offering
> time after time the same sacrifices, which can never
> take away sins;[4] but He, having offered one sacrifice
> for sins for all time, sat down at the right hand of God,
> waiting from that time onward until His enemies be
> made a footstool for His feet. For by one offering He
> has perfected for all time those who are sanctified.

When Jesus called out from the Cross, "It is finished," the work
of redeeming humanity was forever behind Him. He doesn't keep

---

4. Compare with Micah 6:6–8.

coming down from heaven to go through an endless cycle of cruci-fixions. It's over . . . finished . . . done. One sacrifice for all, offered up once for all, so that there might be freedom for all.

If God has, in fact, *perfected* us, as verse 14 indicates, we need to ask ourselves the searching question: "Then why do we work so hard to earn His favor?"

## Benefits to the Believer

We can serve God out of a cringing feeling of failure to measure up, or we can serve Him out of gratitude for the work of grace He has fully brought into our life. Grace is by far a superior motivation to guilt. God doesn't want us running holes in our shoes on some guilt trip. He doesn't want us living life by some Levitical checklist of rules and regulations. He wants us to be free—not just from sin, but from the chafing collar of constraint that the Law clamped around our necks.

God not only wants us to *be* free, He wants us to *live* free, as verses 15–18 indicate.

> And the Holy Spirit also bears witness to us; for after saying,
>> "This is the covenant that I will make
>>> with them
>> After those days, says the Lord:
>> I will put My Laws upon their heart,
>> And upon their mind I will write them,"
> He then says,
>> "And their sins and their lawless deeds
>> I will remember no more."[5]
> Now where there is forgiveness of these things, there
> is no longer any offering for sin.

Having the Law in our hearts as opposed to an external standard of stone is the primary difference between the New Covenant and the Old (Jer. 31:31–33). The power of God's Spirit residing within us is sufficient for us to live life fully, to live life fruitfully, and to live life freely, unfettered from the shackles of sin and from slavery to legalism.

And who in their right mind would go back to any system of slavery once the key had been turned to release them from those shackles?

5. See Jeremiah 31:33–34.

It was for freedom that Christ set us free; therefore
keep standing firm and do not be subject again to a
yoke of slavery. (Gal. 5:1)

 ## *Living Insights*                                           STUDY ONE

Life under the Law is a monotonous routine. It's full of fear and
futility. But we are not under the Law. We are under grace. Look
up Galatians 2:16–21.

- What does this passage teach you about the Law?

_____

_____

_____

_____

Now turn to Galatians 5:16–23.

- What does this passage teach you about the ministry of the Holy
  Spirit?

_____

_____

_____

- What are some attitudes you need to drop to stop living under
  the Law?

_____

_____

_____

- What are some attitudes you need to adopt to start living under
  grace?

_____

_____

_____

*Living Insights*

The core of the New Covenant involves the indwelling of the Holy Spirit.

- Read Romans 8:1–17. List some of the benefits you have because the Spirit is living in you.

_____

_____

_____

_____

_____

- How does the Spirit of God give you help, counsel, and comfort? See John 16:7–13 and Romans 8:26, then give some personal illustrations from your own life.

_____

_____

_____

_____

_____

_____

_____

_____

_____

_____

_____

- Take some time to pray, thanking the Holy Spirit for His ministry in your life and asking Him to empower you to live life fully, fruitfully, and freely.

Chapter 23

# ENTER . . . BUT COME CLEAN

*Hebrews 10:19–25*

The operating room of a hospital is a foreboding place—almost sacred. The air is filtered, pure and clean. The walls and floors are immaculately scrubbed. The instruments are sterilized. A sign hangs over the entrance—Unauthorized Persons: Keep Out.

The only people allowed in the operating room are trained physicians and select hospital personnel. But they, too, must be scrubbed and sterilized, wearing disposable hospital greens with protective masks and foot coverings.

In order for the operating room to fulfill the function for which it was made, it must be free from contamination. Even the smallest of germs can infiltrate and infect the very person who's there for help.

The operating room *is* a special place, set apart for private usage for the most delicate of duties—the saving of human life. The Holy of Holies was a similar type of place. It was the cleanest, most sacred place on earth. It was off-limits to everyone except the high priest, and even he could enter only once a year, on the Day of Atonement. A large, tapestried veil separated the Holy of Holies from the rest of the temple. However, when Jesus died, that curtain was torn from top to bottom (Matt. 27:51). The veil had warned, "Keep out!" but the tearing of the veil tacitly announced, "Come in!" Since the blood of Christ cleansed us from all of sin's contamination, we are now free—not only to enter, but to enter with confidence.

## An Overview of the Passage

Hebrews 10:19–25 falls neatly into outline form. These exhortations make up the section: "let us draw near" (v. 22), "let us hold fast" (v. 23), and "let us consider" (v. 24). All three are built on the foundational facts found in verses 19 and 21, indicated by the causal connective *since.*

> *Since* therefore, brethren, we have confidence to enter the holy place by the blood of Jesus, by a new and living way which He inaugurated for us through the veil, that is, His flesh, and *since* we have a great

155

priest over the house of God, *let us draw near* with a sincere heart in full assurance of faith, having our hearts sprinkled clean from an evil conscience and our bodies washed with pure water. *Let us hold fast* the confession of our hope without wavering, for He who promised is faithful; and *let us consider* how to stimulate one another to love and good deeds, not forsaking our own assembling together, as is the habit of some, but encouraging one another; and all the more, as you see the day drawing near. (vv. 19–25, emphasis added)

## An Explanation of the Passage

In our passage God invites us all—not simply the high priest—to enter the sacred place. To strengthen our steps with confidence, He gives us two facts we can stand on. One, *Jesus' blood has opened the way* (vv. 19–20). Two, *Jesus' presence has filled the house* (v. 21). As a result of the former, we're clean in His presence. As a result of the latter, we're close to His presence.

By way of illustration, those who are allowed to see the work within an operating room have two things in common. One, they must prepare by getting cleaned and scrubbed. Two, they must know the physician, for he is the one who authorizes them to enter the operating room.

The exact definition of *house* in verse 21 has long puzzled expositors. Some interpret it to mean "heaven";[1] others interpret it to mean "the church."[2]

A more satisfying way to approach it, we think, is to view the term as the house of God within each believer. Elsewhere in Scripture, our bodies are referred to as the temple, or house, of God (1 Cor. 6:19, 2 Cor. 6:16, Heb. 3:6). Our physical bodies are analogous to the outer courtyard of His temple, while the soul resides in a holy place deep within. At the moment of salvation, Christ pushes back the veil and fills our spirit—the holiest of places—with His presence.

On the basis of the two facts noted in Hebrews 10:19–21, the writer gives us three commands to obey.

1. For this view, see A *Commentary on the Epistle to the Hebrews,* by Philip Edgcumbe Hughes (Grand Rapids, Mich.: William B. Eerdmans Publishing Co., 1977), pp. 405–10.

2. For this view, see *The Epistle to the Hebrews,* by F. F. Bruce (Grand Rapids, Mich.: William B. Eerdmans Publishing Co., 1964), p. 21; also *The Epistle to the Hebrews,* by Brooke Foss Westcott (Grand Rapids, Mich.: William B. Eerdmans Publishing Co., 1973), p. 321.

First: *Draw near* (v. 22). In this verse the writer exhorts us to crouch down and peek through the keyhole of the house where Christ resides—to see the Lord Jesus at work in the inner recesses of our heart, to get in touch with the presence of God and tap into His power. We are to draw upon *His* adequacy for assuring our faith, cleansing our conscience, and flushing the impurities out of our life.

Second: *Speak out* (v. 23). Notice that our confession centers around hope which is rooted in the promises of a faithful God. Christians who can see God working in their lives, and who have experienced His cleansing and the control of His Spirit, have this hope.

Third: *Stir up* (v. 24). The writer exhorts us to stir up the internal motivation of others—*love*. And he exhorts us to stir that emotion until it spills over into external actions—*good deeds*. In order to do that, we cannot live like islands isolated from each other, but we must pull up close to one another so that we can give encouragement (v. 25).

## A Word of Application

The main thrust of our passage for today is that God invites all of us to enter a sacred place. That place is the deepest level of our being, where He has come to dwell as Lord. Two ideas follow from this truth. One: *It is possible to have a holy place within ourselves.* To any with a poor self-image, that's like finding a gold mine on a seemingly worthless plot of land; it has to cause your property value to soar. Two: *It is impossible to communicate Christ correctly while outside His house.* When we point others to God, we no longer point to a tabernacle made with hands or to the tabernacle of Jesus, who pitched His tent among us so we could see God (John 1:14, 18). Others see God most clearly and most convincingly through the light that radiates from the open windows of His house—from *inside* the lives of those in whom He has taken residence. And as Madeleine L'Engle says:

> We do not draw people to Christ by loudly discrediting what they believe, by telling them how wrong they are and how right we are, but by showing them a light that is so lovely that they want with all their hearts to know the source of it.[3]

Won't you turn your gaze to that light within you and draw from it the confidence and cleansing you need to give you hope? And won't you determine in your heart to be a beacon of light to those around you?

A world that shivers in the darkness will be eternally glad you did.

3. *Walking on Water: Reflections on Faith and Art* (Wheaton, Ill.: Harold Shaw Publishers, 1972), p. 122.

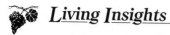

## *Living Insights*

Did you notice the words *faith, hope,* and *love* in Hebrews 10:22–24? This trio appears in other passages in the Bible.

- As you look up these other five passages, record the observations you make based upon the ideas surrounding these three key words.

### Faith, Hope, and Love

1 Corinthians 13:13 _____

_____

_____

Ephesians 1:15–18 _____

_____

_____

Colossians 1:3–6 _____

_____

_____

1 Thessalonians 1:2–3 _____

_____

_____

## *Living Insights*

"Draw near, speak out, stir up!" These commands should not be taken lightly. It would be profitable for us to underscore the importance of these Scriptures in our minds. Let's begin by memorizing Hebrews 10:19–25. First, write out the passage. Then, read it aloud, phrase by phrase, ten times. Now go back and write down as much of it as you can recall. Keep repeating this procedure until you can quote the verses from memory.

- After you have memorized the passage, mull it over in your mind, meditating on its implications for your life.

- Spend some time praying through the passage you've memorized, asking God to give you the insight and initiative necessary to apply it in a personal and specific way.

## Chapter 24

# CHRISTIANS IN CONTRAST

Hebrews 10:26–39

True prophets have always been good at comforting the afflicted and afflicting the comfortable. With gestures like lightning and voices like thunder, they preach with such gale force as to cause the hearts of their audience to shudder.

One such sermon was preached on the afternoon of July 8, 1741, in Enfield, Connecticut. Yet strangely, it was devoid of sweeping gesticulations and thunderous peals of rhetoric. The sermon was delivered by a composed preacher named Jonathan Edwards. Reading calmly from his notes, Edwards spoke on the subject of "Sinners in the Hands of an Angry God." Here are a few of his words.

> There are the black clouds of God's wrath now hanging directly over your heads, full of the dreadful storm and big with thunder; and were it not for the restraining hand of God it would immediately burst forth upon you. The sovereign pleasure of God, for the present, stays His rough wind. Otherwise it would come with fury, and your destruction would come like a whirlwind, and you would be like the chaff of the summer threshing floor.[1]

Like the prophets' words of old, this message swept through the pews and threw people sobbing to the floor in repentance.

Our passage for today, Hebrews 10:26–39, reads like a page from Edwards' sermon, with the prophetic power in its words to change people's lives.

## Review of the Argument

The argument of chapter 10 revolves around Christ inviting us to enter the sacred place within our heart where the Holy Spirit resides. This invitation is based on the two facts found in verses 19–21: One, *Jesus' blood has opened the way;* two, *Jesus' presence has filled the house.* Emanating from these facts are three commands found in verses 22–24: *Draw near, speak out, stir up.*

---

1. Jonathan Edwards, "Sinners in the Hands of an Angry God," *Sermon Classics by Great Preachers,* comp. Peter F. Gunther, rev. ed. (Chicago, Ill.: Moody Press, 1982), pp. 30–31.

In today's passage we find a warning (vv. 26–31), followed by an appeal (vv. 32–38), and then a summary (v. 39).

## Study in Contrast

Verse 39 gives two contrasting categories of people: those who shrink back and those who stand firm. Those who shrink back to destruction are addressed in verses 26–31. Those who stand firm in their faith are addressed in verses 32–38.

### Those Who Shrink

> For if we go on sinning willfully after receiving the knowledge of the truth, there no longer remains a sacrifice for sins, but a certain terrifying expectation of judgment, and the fury of a fire which will consume the adversaries. Anyone who has set aside the Law of Moses dies without mercy on the testimony of two or three witnesses. How much severer punishment do you think he will deserve who has trampled under foot the Son of God, and has regarded as unclean the blood of the covenant by which he was sanctified, and has insulted the Spirit of grace? For we know Him who said, "Vengeance is Mine, I will repay." And again, "The Lord will judge His people." It is a terrifying thing to fall into the hands of the living God. (vv. 26–31)

Question: Who does the "we" in verse 26 refer to? Some say it's the unsaved; others say it's the backslidden believers who've lost their salvation. But one thing is clear—whomever the pronoun refers to, the writer lumps himself in with them. Consequently, it couldn't refer to non-believers. The people referred to have *fully* received "the knowledge of the truth" (v. 26),[2] and they are viewed as the Lord's people (v. 30). So who does this "we" represent?

Answer: It represents those who are genuine believers but whose lives are so carnal they are virtually indistinguishable from non-believers. They are believers who tighten their fists, look God defiantly in the eye, and say, "Leave me alone!"[3] In doing so, they deliberately disregard the lordship of Christ, profaning the blood of the New Covenant, and insulting the Spirit of grace (v. 29).

2. The Greek word translated here as "knowledge" is *epignōsis*. It means "full knowledge," as 1 Timothy 2:4 implies.

3. By the phrase "sinning willfully" in verse 26, the writer means something like the sin of defiance raised in a high-handed manner against God, for which the Mosaic Law provided no pardon (Num. 15:30–31).

Those who shrink back from the grace of God shrink back to their own destruction, just as sinners do when they fall into the hands of an angry God.

God disciplines His children harshly when they continue in willful defiance. And He does so in one of two ways. Either He takes their lives,[4] or He judicially sentences them to live out their lives experiencing the consequences of their sins.[5]

The key to short-circuiting the tragic consequences of defiant sin is to stop dead in our tracks and turn our will toward God, to repent of our carnal lifestyle. Are you somewhere on that willful path leading away from God? In some area of your life, are you raising a defiant fist to God and saying "Stay out . . . leave me alone . . . keep your hands off"? If so, please consider your steps. They follow a precarious path . . . a painful path . . . a path that leads to destruction.

### Those Who Stand

In verses 32–38 the writer changes scenes from the ominous future to the torturous past, from potential divine discipline to actual human persecution.

> But remember the former days, when, after being enlightened, you endured a great conflict of sufferings, partly, by being made a public spectacle through reproaches and tribulations, and partly by becoming sharers with those who were so treated. For you showed sympathy to the prisoners, and accepted joyfully the seizure of your property, knowing that you have for yourselves a better possession and an abiding one. Therefore, do not throw away your confidence, which has a great reward. For you have need of endurance, so that when you have done the will of God, you may receive what was promised.
> For yet in a very little while,
> He who is coming will come, and will not delay.
> But My righteous one shall live by faith;
> And if he shrinks back, My soul has no pleasure in him.

---

4. Compare 1 John 5:16 with Acts 5:1–10 and 1 Corinthians 11:27–30.

5. See 1 Corinthians 3:13–15.

The passage addresses Christians in the midst of mistreatment—Christians who are getting a little shaky but are still standing firm in their faith. They are characterized by several qualities: They are familiar with hardship and pain (vv. 32–33); they are concerned for others in need (v. 34); they are free from materialism (v. 34); and they have confidence in God (vv. 34b–35).

In the earlier scene, the writer afflicted the comfortable; now he comforts the afflicted. The need of the former group is *repentance*; the need of this group is *endurance*.[6]

It's natural to want to rest when the going gets too rough, to retreat when the way gets too rocky. When the incline is steep and we stop for a breather, panting on the side of the road, we don't need a kick in the pants; we need an encouraging word. And that's what the writer gives in verses 37–38. He cheers us up the mountain, telling us to hang in there, that the hike is almost over. And he ends with an arm around our slumped shoulders, affirming us, telling us with an encouraging pat on the back that we're not quitters.

> But we are not of those who shrink back to destruction,
> but of those who have faith to the preserving of the
> soul. (v. 39)

## Questions to Be Answered

The words of a prophet are strong words—words that will either strengthen us to stand firm or cause us to shrink back toward destruction.

Where are you going in your spiritual life? Are you shrinking or standing? What will happen a year from now if you continue on the road you're on? Five years from now? Ten?

Regardless of which group you're in, you have some specific, pressing needs. Either you need repentance to turn you around or you need endurance to keep you on the uphill path of faith. Take a rest stop, won't you, and pray to Him who is able to supply your need beyond what you can even ask or imagine (Eph. 3:20).

---

6. The Greek word is *hupomonē*, a compound of the words *hupo*, meaning "under," and *monē*, meaning "to abide." The idea is to "abide under" or "bear up under" or "remain under" trials, hardships, or burdens. The picture of a donkey or camel bearing up under a heavy load is an accurate picture of what this word means.

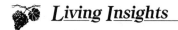

## *Living Insights*

Let's take a breather on our hike through Hebrews to answer the questions posed in the last section of our study for today.

- Where are you going in your spiritual life?

  _____

  _____

- Are you shrinking back from pressure and persecution, or are you standing firm in the faith?

  ☐ Shrinking back

  ☐ Standing but shaking a little at the knees

  ☐ Standing firm

- What will happen a year from now if you continue on the road you're on?

  _____

  _____

  Five years from now?

  _____

  _____

  Ten?

  _____

  _____

- Read the story of the prodigal son in Luke 15:11–24. What two things motivated him to return home to the father who loved him?

  1. _____

  2. _____

- Read Hebrews 10:31 and Romans 2:4. What technique is the Father using to get you to come closer to home?

  _____

  _____

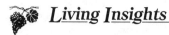

## Living Insights

It's hard to believe that we've already traveled through ten chapters of Hebrews! Take this opportunity to reflect on some of our most noteworthy discoveries.

- We've come to the time for reviewing the key teachings and applications from the lessons we've studied. Jot down what you've learned both in doctrine and in practice.

### Hebrews

A Letter for All Saints and Seasons

Teaching _____

_____

Application _____

_____

_____

### The Last Word

Teaching _____

_____

Application _____

_____

_____

### Angels? Worshipers of the Son

Teaching _____

_____

Application _____

_____

_____

### Don't Neglect! Don't Even Drift!

Teaching _____

_____

Application _____

_____

_____

## Finders Weepers, Losers Keepers

Teaching _____

_____

Application _____

_____

_____

## Perspective on Suffering

Teaching _____

_____

Application _____

_____

_____

## Messiah, Moses, and Me

Teaching _____

_____

Application _____

_____

_____

## Beware of a Hard Heart!

Teaching _____

_____

Application _____

_____

_____

## Stop Churning and Start Resting

Teaching _____

_____

Application _____

_____

## Spiritual Surgery

Teaching _____

_____

Application _____

_____

## A Heavenly Priest for a Needy People

Teaching _____

_____

Application _____

_____

## God's Son—Our Priest

Teaching _____

_____

Application _____

_____

## Let's Grow Up!

Teaching _____

_____

Application _____

_____

_____

## The Peril of Falling Away

Teaching _____

_____

Application _____

_____

_____

## The Brighter Side

Teaching _____

_____

Application _____

_____

_____

## Hope for Those Who Doubt

Teaching _____

_____

Application _____

_____

_____

## Mr. Jones, Meet Melchizedek

Teaching _____

_____

Application _____

_____

_____

## A Permanent Pontifex

Teaching _____

_____

Application _____

_____

_____

## Christ's Covenant . . . New, Never Obsolete

Teaching _____

_____

Application _____

_____

_____

## May I Speak to Your Conscience, Please?

Teaching _____

_____

Application _____

_____

_____

## Signed, Sealed, Delivered . . . in Blood

Teaching _____

_____

Application _____

_____

_____

## One for All, Once for All, Free for All

Teaching _____

_____

Application _____

_____

_____

## Enter . . . but Come Clean

Teaching _____

_____

Application _____

_____

_____

## Christians in Contrast

Teaching _____

_____

Application _____

_____

_____

# BOOKS FOR
# PROBING FURTHER

Like the Shekinah glory that filled the tabernacle, the glory of Christ shines supremely throughout the book of Hebrews. Its radiant shafts extend to every verse, gilding them with a golden touch from heaven.

As we bathe in that luxuriant light, we can't help but see ourselves in a different way. Seeing Jesus lifted up like He is in the book of Hebrews sheds new light on who we are, where we are destined, and how we should live our lives en route.

In the scintillating sparkle of that revelation, we realize that our reason for living is to reflect His glory to a world shrouded in darkness.

The following books have been provided to polish us all for that purpose.

## Commentaries on Hebrews

Bruce, F. F. *The Epistle to the Hebrews.* Grand Rapids, Mich.: William B. Eerdmans Publishing Co., 1964. This volume is part of the excellent series titled The New International Commentary on the New Testament. The research by this prolific scholar is thorough, with the more technical comments relegated to the footnotes.

Gooding, David. *An Unshakeable Kingdom.* Grand Rapids, Mich.: William B. Eerdmans Publishing Co., 1989. In contrast to an exhaustive commentary on the individual verses of Hebrews, this work consists of a series of general introductory studies written in an engaging, personal style. The author concentrates on broad themes and pays special attention to passages of pastoral significance. At the end of each chapter is a list of questions to stimulate group discussion and individual application.

Hughes, Philip Edgcumbe. *A Commentary on the Epistle to the Hebrews.* Grand Rapids, Mich.: William B. Eerdmans Publishing Co., 1977. Although based on the author's research in the original Greek text, this work is easily accessible to the reader who is unfamiliar with the biblical languages. The commentary deals directly with the problem passages of Hebrews and is replete with helpful notes.

## Books about the Tabernacle and Its Symbolism

DeWitt, Roy Lee. *Teaching from the Tabernacle.* Grand Rapids, Mich.: Baker Book House, 1986. This is a thorough but nontechnical work that describes the tabernacle and its symbolism, particularly as it relates to the New Testament. It includes an address to write to for slides of the tabernacle.

Strong, James. *The Tabernacle of Israel: Its Structure and Symbolism.* Grand Rapids, Mich.: Kregel Publications, 1987. This is a scholarly work on the structure and symbolism of the tabernacle that includes illuminating research of the Hebrew terms.

## Books That Tie into Some Key Themes of Hebrews

Henry, Carl F. H. *Christian Countermoves in a Decadent Culture.* Portland, Oreg.: Multnomah Press, 1986. Hebrews exhorted its initial readers to rise above the decadent world in which they lived, and Henry encourages us to do the same, forthrightly discussing the illusions, immorality, and institutions of today's society.

MacDonald, Gordon. *Restoring Your Spiritual Passion.* Nashville, Tenn.: Thomas Nelson Publishers, Oliver Nelson, 1986. Just as Hebrews tries to fan the embers of our faith, so Gordon MacDonald tries to restore the flickering passions of our spiritual life. The book is immensely practical and born out of his own personal experience.

Ortlund, Anne and Ray. *You Don't Have to Quit.* Nashville, Tenn.: Thomas Nelson Publishers, Oliver Nelson, 1988. Quitting is a temptation the Hebrew Christians faced. In a practical book of well-written encouragement, the authors touch upon quitting in all its facets—from quitting school to quitting a marriage to quitting the faith.

Schaeffer, Edith. *Affliction.* Old Tappan, N.J.: Fleming H. Revell Co., 1978. The Hebrew Christians were beset on every side with persecution and affliction. So are many Christians today. Drawing upon a wealth of experience and insight, the author will open your heart to the often painful and difficult ways of God with His people.

Tozer, A. W. *This World: Playground or Battleground?* Camp Hill, Pa.: Christian Publications, 1989. Most people believe we have been put on earth to frolic; Tozer contends we have been put here to fight. His perspective on spiritual warfare is so consistent with the message of Hebrews that it reads almost like a twentieth-century epistle.

# ACKNOWLEDGMENT

Insight for Living gratefully acknowledges permission for the generous use of this excellent source on the book of Hebrews:

Barclay, William. *The Letter to the Hebrews.* Rev. ed. The Daily Study Bible Series. Philadelphia, Pa.: Westminster Press, 1976.

# Insight for Living
## Cassette Tapes
# THE PREEMINENT PERSON OF CHRIST

Like a divine seal, the letter to the Hebrews declares Jesus Christ's position of supremacy. In these profound pages of Scripture, God makes it clear that His Son is preeminent, the one whom all creatures . . . in heaven and on earth . . . should rightfully honor and adore. And what a magnificent example our "merciful and faithful high priest" has set for those who follow Him! By setting aside His glory and becoming a man, He helped us to see the beauty of sacrificial love. At the same time, He showed all creation that He can be trusted with our love and obedience.

| | | | U.S. | Canada |
|---|---|---|---|---|
| PPC | CS | Cassette series—includes album cover .. | **$65.25** | $83.00 |
| | | Individual cassettes—include messages A and B . . . . . . . . . . . . . . . . . . . . . . | 5.00 | 6.35 |

*These prices are subject to change without notice.*

PPC 1-A: *A Letter for All Saints and Seasons*—Survey of Hebrews
B: *The Last Word*—Hebrews 1:1–3

PPC 2-A: *Angels? Worshipers of the Son*—Hebrews 1:4–14
B: *Don't Neglect! Don't Even Drift!*—Hebrews 2:1–4

PPC 3-A: *Finders Weepers, Losers Keepers*—Hebrews 2:5–10
B: *Perspective on Suffering*—Hebrews 2:9–18

PPC 4-A: *Messiah, Moses, and Me*—Hebrews 3:1–6
B: *Beware of a Hard Heart!*—Hebrews 3:7–19

PPC 5-A: *Stop Churning and Start Resting*—Hebrews 4:1–11
B: *Spiritual Surgery*—Hebrews 4:12–13

PPC 6-A: *A Heavenly Priest for a Needy People*—Hebrews 4:14–16
B: *God's Son—Our Priest*—Hebrews 5:1–10

PPC 7-A: *Let's Grow Up!*—Hebrews 5:11–14
B: *The Peril of Falling Away*—Hebrews 6:1–8

PPC 8-A: *The Brighter Side*—Hebrews 6:9–12
B: *Hope for Those Who Doubt*—Hebrews 6:13–20

PPC 9-A: *Mr. Jones, Meet Melchizedek*—Hebrews 7:1–19
B: *A Permanent Pontifex*—Hebrews 7:18–28

PPC 10-A: *Christ's Covenant . . . New, Never Obsolete*—Hebrews 8:1–13
B: *May I Speak to Your Conscience, Please?*—Hebrews 9:1–14

PPC 11-A: *Signed, Sealed, Delivered . . . in Blood*—Hebrews 9:15–28
B: *One for All, Once for All, Free for All*—Hebrews 10:1–18

PPC 12-A: *Enter . . . but Come Clean*—Hebrews 10:19–25
B: *Christians in Contrast*—Hebrews 10:26–39

# How to Order by Mail

Simply mark on the order form whether you want the series or individual tapes. Mail the form with your payment to the appropriate address listed below. We will process your order as promptly as we can.

**United States:** Mail your order to the Sales Department at Insight for Living, Post Office Box 4444, Fullerton, California 92634. If you wish your order to be shipped first-class for faster delivery, add 10 percent of the total order amount (not including California sales tax). Otherwise, please allow four to six weeks for delivery by fourth-class mail. We accept personal checks, money orders, Visa, or MasterCard in payment for materials. Unfortunately, we are unable to offer invoicing or COD orders.

**Canada:** Mail your order to Insight for Living Ministries, Post Office Box 2510, Vancouver, British Columbia V6B 3W7. Please add 7 percent of your total order for first-class postage and allow approximately four weeks for delivery. Our listeners in British Columbia must also add a 6 percent sales tax to the total of all tape orders (not including postage). We accept personal checks, money orders, Visa, or MasterCard in payment for materials. Unfortunately, we are unable to offer invoicing or COD orders.

**Australia, New Zealand, or Papua New Guinea:** Mail your order to Insight for Living, Inc., GPO Box 2823 EE, Melbourne, Victoria 3001, Australia. Please allow six to ten weeks for delivery by surface mail. If you would like your order sent airmail, the delivery time may be reduced. Whether you choose surface or airmail, postage costs must be added to the amount of purchase and included with your order. Please use the chart that follows to determine correct postage. Due to fluctuating currency rates, we can accept only personal checks made payable in U.S. funds, international money orders, Visa, or MasterCard in payment for materials.

**Overseas:** Other overseas residents should contact our U.S. office. Please allow six to ten weeks for delivery by surface mail. If you would like your order sent airmail, the delivery time may be reduced. Whether you choose surface or airmail, postage costs must be added to the amount of purchase and included with your order. Please use the chart that follows to determine correct postage. Due to fluctuating currency rates, we can accept only personal checks made payable in U.S. funds, international money orders, Visa, or MasterCard in payment for materials.

| Type of Postage | Postage Cost |
|---|---|
| Surface | 10% of total order |
| Airmail | 25% of total order |

# For Faster Service, Order by Telephone

To purchase using Visa or MasterCard, you are welcome to use our **toll-free** numbers between the hours of 8:30 A.M. and 4:00 P.M., Pacific time, Monday through Friday. The number to call from anywhere in the United States is **1-800-772-8888.** To order from Canada, call our Vancouver office at **1-800-663-7639.** Vancouver residents should call (604) 272-5811. Telephone orders from overseas are handled through our Sales Department at (714) 870-9161. We are unable to accept collect calls.

## Our Guarantee

Our cassettes are guaranteed for ninety days against faulty performance or breakage due to a defect in the tape. For best results, please be sure your tape recorder is in good operating condition and is cleaned regularly.

**Note:** To cover processing and handling, there is a $10 fee for *any* returned check.

# Order Form

PPC CS represents the entire *The Preeminent Person of Christ* series, while PPC 1–12 are the individual tapes included in the series.

| Series or Tape | Unit Price U.S. | Canada | Quantity | Amount |
|---|---|---|---|---|
| PPC CS | $65.25 | $83.00 | | $ |
| PPC 1 | 5.00 | 6.35 | | |
| PPC 2 | 5.00 | 6.35 | | |
| PPC 3 | 5.00 | 6.35 | | |
| PPC 4 | 5.00 | 6.35 | | |
| PPC 5 | 5.00 | 6.35 | | |
| PPC 6 | 5.00 | 6.35 | | |
| PPC 7 | 5.00 | 6.35 | | |
| PPC 8 | 5.00 | 6.35 | | |
| PPC 9 | 5.00 | 6.35 | | |
| PPC 10 | 5.00 | 6.35 | | |
| PPC 11 | 5.00 | 6.35 | | |
| PPC 12 | 5.00 | 6.35 | | |
| **Subtotal** | | | | |
| **Sales tax** 6% for orders delivered in California or British Columbia | | | | |
| **Postage** 7% in Canada; overseas residents, see "How to Order by Mail" | | | | |
| **10% optional first-class shipping and handling** U.S. residents only | | | | |
| **Gift to Insight for Living** Tax-deductible in the U.S. and Canada | | | | |
| **Total amount due** Please do not send cash. | | | $ | |

If there is a balance:  ☐ apply it as a donation  ☐ please refund

**Form of payment:**

☐ Check or money order made payable to Insight for Living

☐ Credit card (circle one):     Visa     MasterCard

Card Number _____  Expiration Date _____

Signature _____
We cannot process your credit card purchase without your signature.

Name _____

Address _____

City _____  State/Province_____

Zip/Postal Code _____  Country _____

Telephone ( ____ ) _____  Radio Station ___ ___ ___ ___
If questions arise concerning your order, we may need to contact you.

**Mail this order form to the Sales Department at one of these addresses:**
Insight for Living, Post Office Box 4444, Fullerton, CA 92634
Insight for Living Ministries, Post Office Box 2510, Vancouver, BC, Canada V6B 3W7
Insight for Living, Inc., GPO Box 2823 EE, Melbourne, VIC 3001, Australia